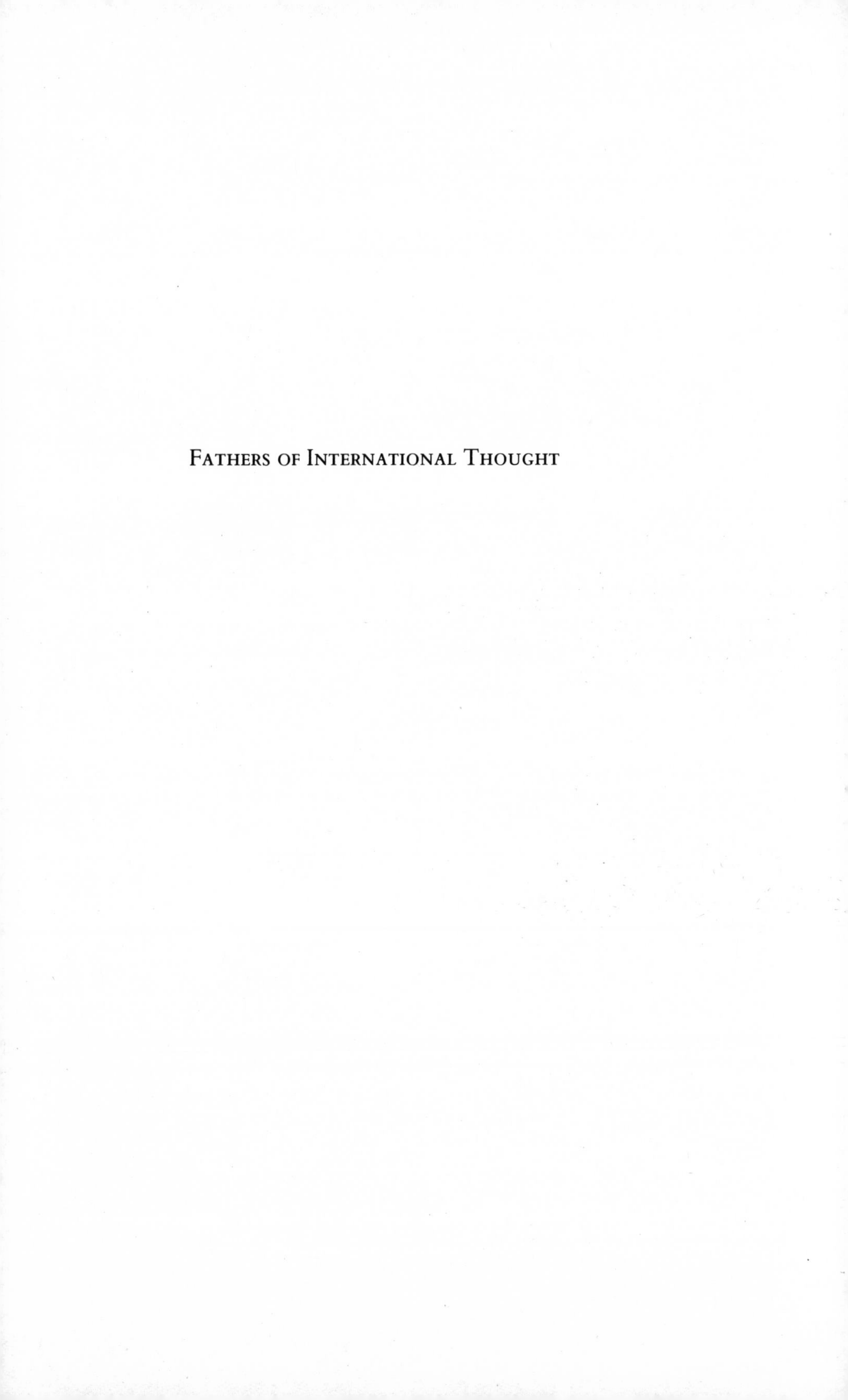

Fathers of International Thought

Kenneth W. Thompson

Fathers of International Thought

The Legacy of Political Theory

Louisiana State University Press
Baton Rouge and London

Manufactured in the United States of America
First printing
03 02 01 00 99 98 97 96 95 94 5 4 3 2 1

Designer: *Glynnis Phoebe*
Typeface: *Bembo*
Typesetter: *G&S Typesetters, Inc.*
Printer and binder: *Thomson-Shore, Inc.*

Library of Congress Cataloging-in-Publication Data

Thompson, Kenneth W., 1921–
Fathers of international thought : the legacy of political theory / Kenneth W. Thompson.
p. cm.
Includes index.
ISBN 0-8071-1905-9 (alk. paper). ISBN 0-8071-1906-7 (pbk.: alk. paper).
1. International relations. 2. Political science. I. Title.
JX1305.T56 1994
327'.01—dc20 93-35872
CIP

The paper in this book meets the guidelines for permanence and durability of the Committee on Production Guidelines for Book Longevity of the Council on Library Resources. ∞

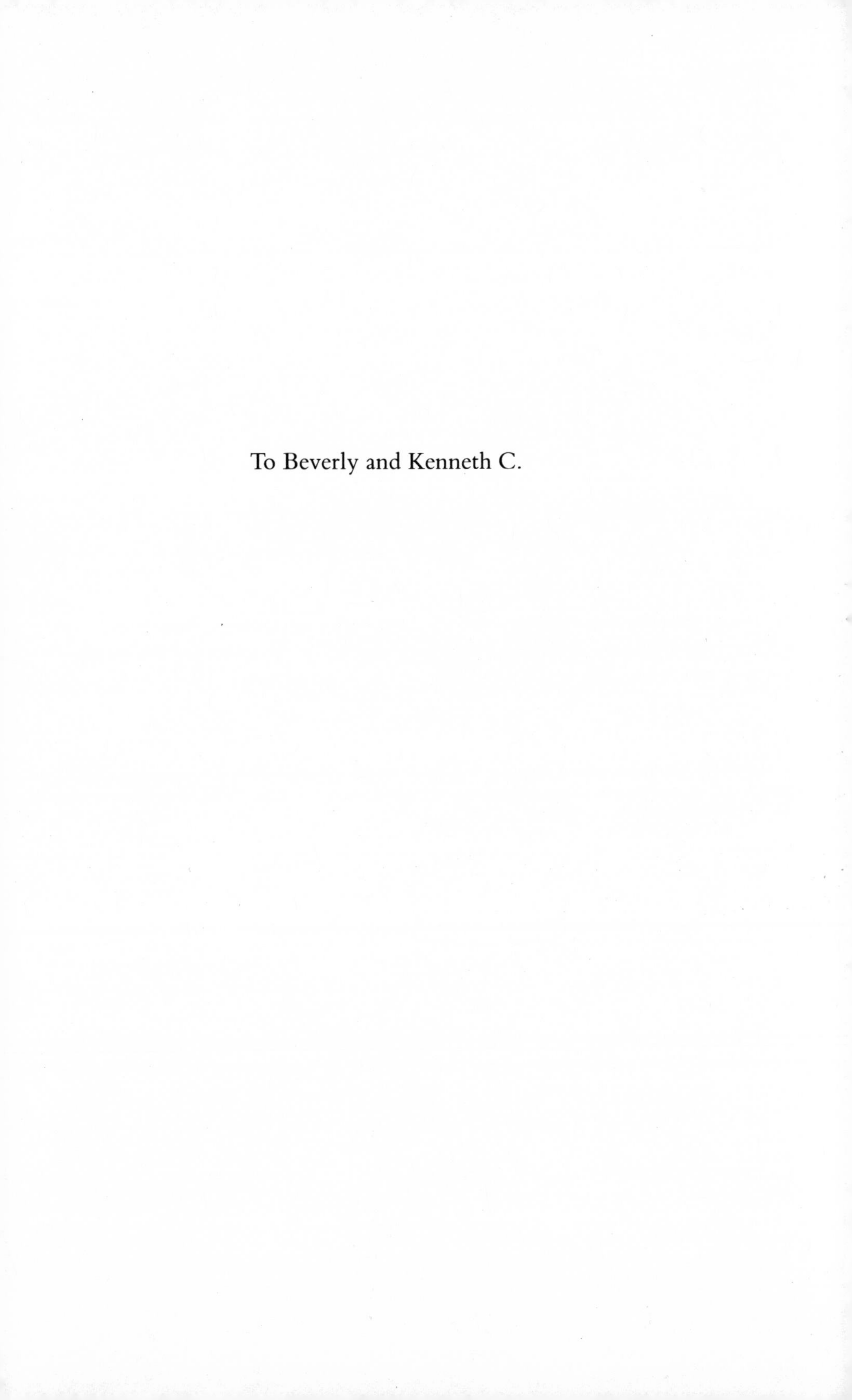

To Beverly and Kenneth C.

Contents

Preface ix

Acknowledgments xiii

Introduction 1

One
Comparing Theories 10

Two
Classical Political Thought 20

Three
Plato (427–347 B.C.) 26

Four
Aristotle (384–322 B.C.) 36

Five
Augustine (A.D. 354–430) 44

Six
Thomas Aquinas (1225–1274) 54

Seven
Niccolò Machiavelli (1469–1527) 62

Eight
The Seventeenth Century
Grotius (1583–1645) 69
Thomas Hobbes (1588–1679) 76
John Locke (1632–1704) 80

NINE
The Eighteenth Century
Adam Smith (1723–1790) 84
David Hume (1711–1776) 89
Charles-Louis de Secondat, baron de Montesquieu (1689–1755) 94
Jean-Jacques Rousseau (1712–1778) 94
Edmund Burke (1729–1797) 98

TEN
The Nineteenth Century
Immanuel Kant (1724–1804) 104
Georg Wilhelm Friedrich Hegel (1770–1831) 113
Karl Marx (1818–1883) 120

EPILOGUE 127

BIBLIOGRAPHY 131

INDEX 141

Preface

The present volume is a companion piece to *Masters of International Thought: Major Twentieth-Century Theorists and the World Crisis*. In that volume, I tried to identify and analyze the thinking of some eighteen leading twentieth-century thinkers. Almost half of the eighteen were alive when I completed the work. Today only three remain with us, yet students of international relations continue to revisit and evaluate the writings of the fifteen who have departed no less than those of the three master thinkers who are still on the scene (John H. Herz, George F. Kennan, and Louis J. Halle, Jr.).

Observers note that debates over the validity of Hans J. Morgenthau's concept of power politics and the national interest are as lively and intense as when he wrote. Reinhold Niebuhr remains the towering figure in normative thinking on international relations (I remember Walter Lippmann saying about Niebuhr at a conference in which they both participated, "How many generations will it be before we shall see his equal?"). For his part, Lippmann has left an empty chair as America's premier diplomatic columnist and political philosopher. For those who question the value of studying "the thoughts of dead men," the literature of international relations theory provides an answer to their doubts.[1]

1. Charles H. Hyneman was the guiding spirit in the early 1950s of a restructuring of political science at Northwestern University. In that task, he challenged the continued teaching of political theory, saying "Why study dead men?" Ironi-

The writings of E. H. Carr, David Mitrany, Quincy Wright, John Courtney Murray, Nicholas J. Spykman, Arnold Wolfers, Herbert Butterfield, Martin Wight, Charles de Visscher, and Raymond Aron are as important in the 1990s as they were in the 1970s and 1980s. It can be argued that if Presidents Reagan and Bush in the 1980s and 1990 had read and understood the writings of thinkers such as Spykman and Morgenthau before allowing the Middle East balance of power to shift so decisively to Saddam Hussein's Iraq, the Gulf crisis might have been averted.

Masters of International Thought throws a powerful light on another issue. Sir Alfred North Whitehead once said that all political thought since Plato is a footnote. Readers of *Masters* will find recurrent evidence that most of the eighteen thinkers discussed there discovered points of contemporary relevance in certain "fathers" of political and international thought. Niebuhr acknowledged the decisive influence of Augustine on his thought. Father Murray went back to Aquinas. Butterfield took inspiration from German and British historiography. Morgenthau paid homage to Aristotle, Max Weber, Friedrich Nietzsche, and Bismarck. Toynbee read Oswald Spengler, Henri Bergson, Edward Gibbon, and E. A. Freeman. In a particularly vivid expression, Toynbee spoke of the need for any historian or thinker "to stand on the shoulders of those who had gone before him."

The present volume, *Fathers of International Thought,* attempts to trace the thinking of those who have provided the supporting shoulders for the master thinkers. More often than not, the influence of one thinker on another is hidden from view. The influence may be indirect. The sharing of ideas is a complex process. It was said of Niebuhr that his mind resembled a meat grinder. He took fragments of thought from a vast array of sources and ground them together into new combinations of principles and conclusions. For thinkers such as Niebuhr and Murray, the sources of their thought were more often classical than contemporary. At the University of Chicago, Morgenthau offered a seminar for many years on the contemporary relevance of Aristotle. Lippmann's last important treatise, *The Public Philosophy,* called for the rediscovery of natural law. While the use that the masters made of their pre-

cally, political scientists continue to read Hyneman's work, especially *Bureaucracy in Democracy,* as well as Plato and Artistotle.

decessors varied from thinker to thinker, the interconnections between earlier and modern thought is too apparent to be denied, as illustrated in discussions of Hobbes and Locke by Wolfers or of Grotius, Kant, and Machiavelli by Wight.

This book intends no comprehensive and authoritative analysis of "the greats" in political theory. Rather, the focus is on the contemporary relevance of their thought for international politics and international relations. Purists may question the use of the classics in this way. Our inquiry's goal, however, is to test and explore whether the writings of some sixteen political theorists whom we call the fathers clarify and illuminate in new and different ways the recurrent issues of our world.

ACKNOWLEDGMENTS

I am much indebted to my colleague and friend Dante Germino of the Department of Government and Foreign Affairs at the University of Virginia. During most of the past decade and a half, we have taught a joint course called "The Philosophy of International Relations." In it we sought to combine the approaches of the political theorist and the theorist of international relations. We have been alone for some years in offering the course. I have learned much from Professor Germino about individual political theorists throughout our association.

I am equally grateful to my outstanding secretary, Shirley Kohut. No one could be more fortunate than I have been to have her assistance during the past fifteen years. She has been tireless in performing a wide range of duties and unrivaled in her ability to take initiative. Her skill and productivity as a secretary are matched only by her patience in coping with my eccentricities. My gratitude for her help and goodwill is unbounded.

Finally, I am greatly indebted to Marshal Zeringue and Jeff Vogelgesang for their assistance in the later stages of preparation of this manuscript.

Fathers of International Thought

Introduction

This is a book on great thinkers. I propose to call them the fathers of political and international thought. It is clear that burden of proof rests with anyone making such a proposal. As we shall see, different schools of thought offer different interpretations and draw different conclusions concerning the relationship between political theory and international thought. The one way to throw light on this issue is to examine the thought of the fathers and the group I have called the masters in another published work.[1] This involves reading the texts of the fathers as though one were an interrogator. Our intention is to ask questions such as What do the fathers say about the relationship of states and peoples? Is there a concept of a wider society, whether national or ethnic, regional or what moderns call the international society? Does sovereignty reside in the states or in the wider society? Or are the people sovereign and is the individual ultimately the source of sovereignty? Did the fathers write in a time of crisis and far-reaching change? How are we to characterize their thought?

All of this prompts a further question: Why study the philosophers of politics and international relations? I suggest several answers to this question. First, the study of politics and international relations tends to become a frantic shuttling back and forth between crises. What we need most—citizens and policy makers—is

1. Kenneth W. Thompson, *Masters of International Thought: Major Twentieth-Century Theorists and the World Crisis* (Baton Rouge, 1980).

a change of pace. To take but one example, in the year 1991 we witnessed Iraq's invasion of Kuwait, the Gulf War, the freeing of Kuwait, Saddam Hussein's threat to the Kurds and the Shiites, the proclamations about Europe 1992, the declaration of independence by Croatia and Slovenia, the Soviet coup in August, the abortive and short-lived union of former Soviet states followed by the Commonwealth of Independent States and therefore newly independent states, the unremitting conflict in the former Yugoslavia, the call for Americans to turn inward, and the threat of a U.S.-Japan trade war. World politics is "too much with us early and late." The hard-pressed individual looks for some Archimedean point from which to view the world, to help distinguish what is transient from what is permanent. We need time for contemplation, which is the essence of philosophy. Busy policy makers cry out for time to think, reflect, and reach judgments. If not all, at least some policy makers recognize this need as paramount.

Second, philosophy is sometimes defined as "an unusually stubborn attempt to think clearly." It is the search for ideas and concepts, principles and propositions. They are among the tools that can enhance clearer thinking and analysis. Tocqueville found that Americans tend not to be philosophical or reflective. They treat problems on the surface without penetrating underlying assumptions and forces.

Third, philosophy is an effort to take hold of stubborn realities. The scientist has a laboratory where he withdraws from the urgencies of society. Shielded from the world, he seeks to cure cancer, to grow miracle rice, or to control pollution. In a certain sense, philosophy is the laboratory of the human scientist. It involves what Toynbee calls a process of "withdrawal and return." In American politics, analysts speak of in-and-outers. Fourth, philosophy or theory is an effort to give order and meaning to a body of seemingly unrelated data. Without philosophy, wisdom is lost in knowledge and knowledge is swallowed up in information.

What, then, is the place of a philosophical approach to our subject? In the 1950s and 1960s, a score of political thinkers in the United States and Great Britain contributed in fundamental ways to international theory. Prominent among them was Hans J. Morgenthau, whose graduate seminar on the philosophy of international relations at the University of Chicago inspired students to search for the underlying sources of conflict. While Morgenthau's lectures never led to a separate publication, he often suggested a volume was needed that would introduce the major thinkers whose work could be called philosophical. He had in mind especially theorists such as Reinhold Niebuhr, Walter Lippmann, and Louis J. Halle, Jr., who had exerted important influences on contemporary thinking.

With Morgenthau's encouragement, I prepared the text *Masters of International Thought* with concise summations of the philosophies of eighteen significant writers. Individual chapters took the form of personal and intellectual profiles. What distinguished the eighteen master thinkers from many other students of international relations was the breadth and generality of their thought. Almost without exception, they sought to link contemporary international relations thinking with traditional and modern political theory. Plato and Aristotle, Augustine and Aquinas, Machiavelli and Hobbes, and Adam Smith and Grotius provided the foundations for these contemporary thinkers about man, politics, and society. Because the core problems in the philosophy of international relations concerned power and morality, authority and order, and justice and equality, not surprisingly modern theorists invoked the classical political philosophers. While not every master thinker linked his thought as closely with earlier philosophers as Niebuhr did with Augustine or Murray with Aquinas, a returning to the classics was a defining characteristic of virtually every one of the eighteen thinkers. For this reason their work is appropriately designated "philosophy of international relations." Technical international law studies and the institutional analysis that characterized much writing on international organizations paid less attention to philosophical issues. Indeed, one behavioral political scientist scornfully remarked that political philosophy was irrelevant because it concentrated on "the writings of dead men" who presumably had little to say about the present. The masters of international relations set out to refute this critical view of political theory.

What was it about the postwar period that generated such interest in political philosophy? How are we to account for the revival of philosophy as an approach to international relations? First, World War II and its aftermath were factors. The migration of European thinkers before and during the war had a profound impact. Earlier scientists and scholars in search of freedom and seeking more rewarding personal and professional lives abroad had migrated to the United States, as had intellectuals of widely differing national origins. Viewed in the context of successive waves of migration, however, few if any social movements can match the one occurring in the 1930s and 1940s with the flight of intellectuals from Hitler's Germany. Some found their way directly into science and government and others into business and academic life. It is fair to say that the Manhattan Project housed under Stagg Field at the University of Chicago and leading to the discovery of the atomic bomb would not have been possible without European scientists. In the humanities and social sciences, the graduate school of the New School for Social Research in New York provided an academic home for some of the best minds of Europe, including Leo Strauss, Hans Spier, Arnold Brecht, Kurt Riessler, Hans Jonas, and Erich Hula. Many of the most original thinkers in the social sciences in postwar America were refugees from Hitler's Germany and are esteemed to this day for their courage and original contributions to American social thought.

No field or discipline profited more from this migration of talent than international studies and certain related sectors of political thought. One group constituted the most important figures in political philosophy: Leo Strauss, Hannah Arendt, Hans Jonas, and Eric Voegelin. Another comprised major theorists of comparative government: Carl Joachim Friedrich, Franz and Sigmund Neumann, Otto Kirchheimer, Chancellor Bruning, and Waldemar Gurian. The study of international law received new impetus from Leo Gross and Hans Kelsen. Other legal scholars remained in England, including George Schwarzenberger and Hersh Lauterpacht, and still others chose to continue their work in Spain and Switzerland. History, sociology, economics, and literature claimed their share of leading European thinkers, among them Jacob Viner, Friedrich von Hayek, Karl Mannheim, and Joseph A. Schumpeter. It would be difficult, if not impossible, to find a comparable migration of human talent in all of intellectual history. Fortunately, American universities were generally receptive to influences from those German, British, and European scholars who were most sympathetic to philosophical approaches. As graduate students in the early postwar period, my fellow students and I partook of a veritable intellectual feast at the University of Chicago served up by philosophers who were part of this migration.

I cannot think of a situation before or since that is comparable to what happened in the immediate postwar years.

Second, the nature of international politics invited an approach more attuned to an understanding of the historic relations among independent and sovereign political units. European-American and certain British scholars insisted on a world view that emphasized the importance of power in politics. For nearly two centuries, Americans had been shielded from the harsh realities of power politics because of the nation's isolation from Europe and the surrogate role played by the British navy in protecting U.S. ships and interests, particularly across the seaways of the Atlantic. By contrast, Britain and the states of Europe for nearly four hundred years had lived with the reality of power politics. For them, as for the founding fathers (who were children of European thought), power was seen as a perennial factor in government and politics unlikely to disappear even with a new international order. Postwar Americans were more often children of Woodrow Wilson in his reformist and evangelical phase and were therefore more optimistic about international law and organization as substitutes for power politics. In opposition to much of European thought, Wilsonians prophesied that archaic international political practices such as alliances and the balance of power were everywhere being replaced by new institutional structures reflecting the common interests of mankind.

Not surprisingly, the continuing interrelation between the reformist view of international relations and the more newfangled behavioral approaches to political science, on one hand, and the historic European view of international society and traditional political philosophy on the other, persisted through most of the mid-twentieth century. Therefore, those European-Americans who maintained that power was a perennial reality were also those who clung to the concepts and methods of political philosophy. Thus Reinhold Niebuhr could describe Arnold Wolfers as more a political philosopher than a political scientist. Writing in the preface to the latter's *Discord and Collaboration: Essays on International Politics,* Niebuhr observed: "He is a 'philosopher' in that he scrutinizes and weighs the validity of various theories, concepts and presuppositions and discusses the larger patterns of international relations. But as any good philosopher, he is also a scientist in the sense that empirically ascertained facts serve him as the final criteria for the adequacy of general concepts or for the validity of general suppositions." For both Niebuhr and Wolfers philosophy was joined with politics and power in theorizing. Niebuhr put it this way: "The issues discussed by Dr. Wolfers are by no means 'academic.' They go to the heart of many of the burning problems of contemporary foreign relations." Or as his former students summarized Wolfers' contribution: He "has excelled in making theory relevant to policy and in making the analysis of policy yield insights that further refine theory."[2]

Third, the normative perspective is central to the philosophy of international relations and has occupied a conspicuous place in the philosophical approach of the postwar period. For those approaches that were dominant in the first half of the twentieth century, the normative question had been considered and presumably been answered. Later thinkers were more uncertain. In its simplest form, normative thinking entails an inquiry into the "is" and the "ought" of political relationships. The "ought" in the first four decades of the century was unquestionably internationalism and international law and organization. Observers of the international scene thought in terms of "good internationalism" (the League of Nations) and "bad nationalism" (Hitler's Germany). Few if any thinkers concerned themselves with "bad internationalism" (the quest for domination by the Communist International) or "good nationalism" (the Good Neighbor Policy).

If we look back to the thinkers who sought to return normative thinking to its historic and philosophic moorings, the majority are philosophers of international relations. Niebuhr, Morgenthau, and Sir Herbert Butterfield undertook to instruct their contemporaries on the complexities of moral choice, mirroring Justice Oliver Wendell Holmes's cryptic observation that some people admired the man of principle but he respected the man who could find his way through a maze of conflicting moral principles. In a word, values interact and compete. In international relations, the goals of peace and order compete, as do stability and change. Domestically, freedom of speech and assembly, as the Supreme Court

2. Arnold Wolfers, *Discord and Collaboration: Essays on International Politics* (Baltimore, 1962), viii; Roger Hilsman and Robert C. Good, eds., *Foreign Policy in the Sixties: The Issues and the Instruments: Essays in Honor of Arnold Wolfers* (Baltimore, 1965), xi.

decreed, give no one the right to cry "Fire!" in a crowded theater. Moral judgments by national leaders in foreign relations are often premature, in part because of what Butterfield described as the idolatrous worship of some superperson, society, state, or other large-scale organization. Normative thinking for Butterfield requires walking alongside the actors in history, placing oneself in their shoes, seeking to recapture their perception of events, and striving to understand the problems with which they had to cope and the standards they sought to uphold.

Opposed to normative thinking is the tendency for every contemporary leader to be locked into systems of national self-righteousness, which make the weighing of choices in a process of moral reasoning ever more difficult. When Butterfield founded the British Committee on the Theory of International Politics, he stated its purpose as being the *study* of "the nature of the international state-system, the assumptions and ideas of diplomacy, the principles of foreign policy, *the ethics of international relations and war* [my emphasis]." He explained that the committee's concern was more "with the historical than the contemporary, with the normative than the scientific, with the philosophical than the methodological, with principles than with policy." Sustaining the work of the committee was a pervasive moral concern that he summarized thus: "The underlying aim . . . is to clarify the principles of prudence and moral obligation which have held together the international society of states throughout its history, and still hold it together." The international realm is the political order of "the contingent and the unforeseen, in which the survival of nations may be at stake, and agonizing decisions have to be made."[3]

For the children of World War II, the philosophy of international relations strengthened their capacity to cope with the postwar world. For most returning service personnel, one illusion had given way to another along the path to greater understanding of the world. American innocence about the world led some to assume we could have as much or as little to do with the world as we chose. It would be possible to accept responsibility for the defense of vital interests or to remain aloof following the ending of a great war much as we had embraced isolationism before the con-

3. Herbert Butterfield and Martin Wight, eds., *Diplomatic Investigations: Essays in the Theory of International Politics* (Cambridge, Mass., 1966), 11, 12, 13.

flict broke out. An opposite illusion was belief in the American Century, wherein the writ of the United States would be spread throughout the world. From the illusion that we could abstain from the practice of power politics, we embarked on a postwar crusade to establish and maintain democracy everywhere through a new American role as world policeman. Having denounced alliances and the balance of power, we had by the mid-1950s negotiated some forty separate security pacts with nations around the globe.

The function of a philosophical viewpoint of international relations has been to help balance illusions and possibilities, innocence and hope. If philosophy is defined as an unusually stubborn attempt to think clearly, then a comprehensive philosophical approach to world politics should lead to the rediscovery of our place in history. Perhaps that is why so many who served in a worldwide crusade to subdue Hitler and Japan and returned to a nation bent on achieving a utopian world order turned to the philosophy of international relations. It enabled them to exchange renewed hope for profound anxiety. Having moved from illusion to disillusionment, Americans whose maturing had occurred in the midst of war regained some modicum of confidence through this wider approach to international relations.

The lessons from this experience are that philosophy and intellectual history can be relevant to the study of international politics and that modern-day thinking will more likely flourish if rooted in philosophies of the past. One strength of the philosophical approach is its relative immunity from fads and fashions in an ever-changing present. Further, philosophy also provides a grounding for the examination of such perennial issues as power and morality or peace and order. These foundations are vital when the temptation is ever present to turn to nostrums and panaceas to relieve the gravity of harsh conflicts. In recent times, proponents of far-reaching changes in the international system have argued, "Change x is necessary and is therefore possible." A reexamination of philosophies is a hedge against wishful thinking.

The other contribution from the past is that of first-rate minds grappling with the grave issues of war and peace. A former president of Brown University, Henry Wriston, was wont to say: "First-class problems attract first-class minds." As the history of thought makes clear, the fathers and the master thinkers have contributed in this way. Therefore, we ought to return to their work to reinvigorate present thinking as we confront a whole universe of challenging new problems.

One

Comparing Theories

The proponents of three viewpoints on the contemporary relevance of the fathers of political theory for international thought have vied with one another for recognition and approval since the mid-twentieth century. According to the first viewpoint, traditional political theory is inextricably linked with the idea of the state. The state is central to political theory. Because no universal state exists in international relations, political theory has little to say about international problems. The second viewpoint acknowledges the cleavage between political theory and international thought but attributes it to mutual neglect, political theory for international theory and international theory for political theory. For English-speaking theorists, history points to the unique political experience of England and the United States. The third viewpoint starts from assumptions similar to those of the first but argues that problems such as authority, freedom, order, community, justice, and political unity—manifested historically within a diversity of political systems—are present also in international relations. Each of these views deserves our attention as we set out on the search for the basic elements in a philosophy of international relations.

The first viewpoint is well expressed by Martin Wight in an unusually provocative paper entitled "Why Is There No International Theory?"[1] A highly respected professor of international re-

1. Martin Wight, "Why Is There No International Theory?" in Herbert Butterfield and Martin Wight, eds., *Diplomatic Investigations: Essays in the Theory of International Politics* (Cambridge, Mass., 1966), 17–34.

lations at the London School of Economics, Wight, whose life was cut short in his fifties and a substantial part of whose work has been published posthumously from his lecture notes, wrote of the essential disharmony between international theory and diplomatic practice and the resistance of the subject matter to theorizing. According to Wight, theory requires the language of law and political theory, but law and political theory presuppose more predictable and ordered relationships than are possible in a half-ordered, half-anarchic international society. The goal in political theory is the good life. Man strives within the state for self-realization and the attainment of virtue. The goal for the actors in international theory who represent the nation-state is survival. In political theory revolution is the extreme case and the exception, but in international theory force or violence is the rule.

In three areas of international relations—wartime devastation and pillage, nuclear threats, and intervention to defend oppressed minorities—the language of political theory is found wanting as a description of international reality unless, of course, the prevailing disorder within some nations comes to characterize all nation-states. Wight recognizes the diversity of international relations, saying: "It is necessary to see the domain of international theory stretching all the way from the noble attempt of Grotius and his successors to establish the laws of war at one extreme, to de Maistre's 'occult and terrible law' of the violent destruction of the human species at the other."[2] Wight argues that international politics is not the domain of political theory.

Some writers acknowledge the existence of strife and violence in international relations but ask, What about the modern city? What about drugs and random violence, race riots and gang wars, in the inner cities of the United States? Here political and international theories diverge in their management of conflict and strife. For individuals, movement from a lawless state of nature to security under a sovereign state requires a social contract. Theorists of differing political philosophies agree on the institutionalizing of political order. On the necessity for finding an escape from the state of nature, Hobbes and Locke, however far-reaching their differences, are in substantial accord. By contrast, for sovereign nation-states international anarchy is the manifestation of a state

2. *Ibid.*, 33.

of nature that is "not intolerable." Nation-states have learned to live with strife and violence.

International disorder is evidently a corollary of national sovereignty. However, the lack of a social contract among states, according to Samuel Pufendorf, doesn't necessarily lead to "those inconveniences which are attendant upon a pure state of nature." Emmerich von Vattel explains the differences thus: "Individuals are so constituted that they could accomplish but little by themselves and could scarcely get on without the assistance of civil society and its law. But as soon as a sufficient number have united under a government, they are able to provide for most of their needs, and they find the help of other political societies not so necessary to them as the state itself is to individuals."[3]

The differences between political and international theory are manifest in other ways. According to Wight, the classical interpreters of politics are the political philosophers, whereas those of international relations constitute a rather amorphous body of thinkers representing at least six different approaches to the international community. The first of these is international law, or what has been called "an amalgam of formulae, jurisprudence, political speculation and recorded practice."[4] Traditional international law has roots in the public law of eighteenth-century Europe. The second approach involves reformist writings on new concepts and institutions of international relations, those that set the stage for the League of Nations. Representatives of this school are described as irenists, or men "full of anger and wrath." Their anger is addressed to the need for international government. They include Erasmus, Sully, William Penn, the Abbé de St. Pierre, and Crucé. Having identified the reformist school, Wight goes on to characterize its members as "not rich in ideas." The third approach is represented by realists, or proponents of *raison d'état,* as discussed by Friedrich Meinecke in his wide-ranging book *Machiavellianism.* The majority of the early realists were writers "notable in another sphere": statesmen such as Frederick the Great, philosophers such as Hegel and Fichte, and historians like Ranke and Treitschke. Wight suggests that what these writers intended to convey is for the most part accessible only to scholars, although

3. Quoted *ibid.,* 31.
4. Quoted *ibid.,* 18.

others might debate his conclusion. Machiavelli is of course the most conspicuous exception. The fourth approach, according to Wight, is more rewarding as a source of international thought than any of the others, except perhaps international law. It is embodied by a select group of philosophers, political philosophers, and historians, the authors of a tradition that lives on into the late twentieth century. Their contributions, while fragmentary, are enduring and include David Hume's essay "The Balance of Power," Jean-Jacques Rousseau's *Project of Perpetual Peace,* Edmund Burke's *Thought on French Affairs* and *Letters on a Regicide Peace*, Ranke's essay "The Great Powers," and John Stuart Mill's essay on the law of nations. Yet except for Burke, and in another connection Machiavelli, all these thinkers were primarily political, not international, theorists. Their international writings came almost as an afterthought. The fifth approach is represented by memoirs, speeches, and dispatches of statesmen and diplomats such as Otto von Bismarck, Lord Salisbury, Canning, and some of the founders of the American republic. The historians Thucydides, Sir John Seeley, and Garrett Mattingly exemplify the last approach. They wrote narrative history but history that was based on certain underlying propositions and concerns as illustrated in Thucydides' writings in the Melian dialogue.

Still other distinctions deserve attention. Political theory is progressivist, whereas international politics has historically been a realm of recurrence and repetition. In international theory, "conviction precedes the evidence" (something E. H. Carr illustrates when he explains that usually some utopian goal precedes the creation of a science, as when the need for bridges and harbors comes before the study of engineering). World government is necessary; therefore, it is possible. By contrast, political theory reflects the more immediate facts; its links are with political experience. Political theory has a direct relationship with political activity. By comparison, international law displays an inverse relationship with international politics. A sometime diplomatic historian writes: "When diplomacy is violent and unscrupulous," international law turns to precepts of natural or higher law (witness Nuremberg). When diplomacy is closer to reality, "international law crawls in the mud of legal positivism."[5] If Thomas More were to

5. Quoted *ibid.*, 29.

return to the world he knew in the sixteenth century, he would find the international realm much the same but a sovereign state such as England substantially altered. The world of politics and political theory is subject to transformation by society, the state, and the individual. For the majority of political theorists, international politics has been seen as nothing more than "an untidy fringe" of domestic politics. Until recently international theory has usually remained a concluding chapter or last-minute supplement in political theory textbooks intended primarily for a handful of interested students. International theory has remained an orphan in the larger family of organized political thought.

The second viewpoint on the seeming divorce between political theory and international theory explains the division as the result of mutual neglect and reflects the unique experiences of England and the United States. Arnold Wolfers, the respected Sterling Professor of International Relations at Yale University in the 1950s and early 1960s, begins his formative essay "Political Theory and International Relations" with the assertion: "Nowhere in English-speaking countries would the study of government and politics be considered complete that did not include political theory." Down to the present day, political theory is seen as the core of the discipline political science. However, the interconnections between political theory and international relations are tenuous, fragile, and sometimes obscure. In courses on political theory, Wolfers finds that students hear little or nothing about foreign policy. Matching this neglect, the student is rarely exposed to earlier political thinkers in courses in international or comparative politics. In England and the United States in particular, what are the reasons for the separation, if not the divorce, between the two fields, and what are the prospects for a "remarriage"?

Wolfers discovers one reason for the separation in the dominance of Wilsonian idealism on the American academic scene after World War I. In this era, the goal of international relations was a crusade on behalf of peace and international cooperation through the newly created League of Nations (intellectuals harbored a sense of guilt because the U.S. Senate rejected the League). Because the initial emphasis was on the "ought" rather than the "is" of the international political order, students turned to reformist thinkers such as Kant, Sully, William Penn, and Jeremy Bentham and their peace plans, ignoring realist thinkers such as Machiavelli and Hobbes.

In the 1950s, normative and causal theorizing took a new lease on life. A reaction set in against some of the too-narrow empirical and scientific approaches. Intellectual and social tendencies prepared the groundwork for a renewed emphasis on normative thought. Some normative theorists who called themselves consequentialists predicted undesirable consequences if their political norms and axioms were not followed. Earlier thinkers were invoked to illustrate causal reasoning. For example, Alexander Hamilton's admonition not to continue wars to the point of the enemy's surrender if compromise is possible is based on the proposition that unconditional surrender will make the resulting peace less secure. Hume's essay on the balance of power offers another example. In describing its importance Wolfers asserts: "While Hume can be said to imply that governments should aim at balanced power in the world, his reasoning is based on generalizations concerning the way states as a rule have behaved in the past and are likely to behave in the future."[6] Here the connection between political and international theory is made apparent.

According to Wolfers, what most political theorists offer are "broad assumptions" about man and his nature. Thus they provide important "starting points" for thinking about the social forces that are a reflection of human nature. Their contributions are more often normative than strictly empirical. They are seeking to decide such issues as "when it is right or wrong to participate in 'other people's wars,' to interfere in the domestic affairs of others, to keep faith with allies, or to expand into new territory." Such thinkers clearly have relevance for today's global questions, although some writers argue that ideologies, technologies, and interdependencies have transformed the international system. Wolfers adds: "They were also concerned with what they called the prudence of certain types of action, prudence meaning expediency guided and moderated by morality and reason."[7]

6. Arnold Wolfers, *The Anglo-American Tradition in Foreign Affairs: Readings from Thomas More to Woodrow Wilson,* ed. Arnold Wolfers and Laurence W. Martin (New Haven, 1956), xi.

7. *Ibid.,* xiii.

Moreover, not only do normative concerns argue for the connection between political activity on the domestic and international scenes, but so do some of the more novel developments of the twentieth century. The common character of the domestic and the international arenas is not the result of the greater lawfulness and order made possible by international government, as Wilson had hoped, but stems more often from "tyrannical suppression and persecution" and "revolutionary strife," which have spread across much of the world. Far-reaching changes in the problems and patterns of governance make more appropriate the quest for a comprehensive theory of politics that does justice to both national and international politics, to stability and instability, and to semi-anarchy and order.

Wolfers goes on, however, to contrast and identify points of similarity and difference between domestic and international politics by introducing the concept of "moral opportunity." In the four centuries of the modern state system, England, the United States, and certain other Western countries have forged institutions of constitutional government and civil liberty under which human development is enhanced. By contrast, many of the states that make up international society have known only unremitting rivalry and war (Poland is a leading example). Not surprisingly, political philosophers have viewed the "internal scene" as an "opportunity" for the pursuit of the good life, or virtue as Aristotle described it, whereas the "external" realm has more often appeared to be an arena of frustration and disappointment. Wolfers sums up the differences in question-conclusion form. Is it any wonder that students of political theory should be more interested in how "theorists of the past . . . helped to solve the problems of government at home than in what they had to say about the comparatively barren and stagnant power politics of the multistate system?" He makes plain the reasons when he writes, "There cannot fail to be a difference in 'moral opportunity' between a realm in which every nation is at the mercy of the acts of others and one in which the course of events is predominantly shaped by its own decision."[8]

Having suggested that modern international relations were unknown in the Roman Empire once it had conquered most of

8. *Ibid.*, xvii.

its neighbors and in medieval Christendom when the primary struggle was between emperor and pope, Wolfers calls attention to the reappearance in the twentieth century of overlapping loyalties. Rivalries have manifested themselves both at the secular and sacerdotal levels. Having asked whether Augustine, Aquinas, or Dante has any relevance for our times, Wolfers then identifies what he describes as the "new medievalism." He writes, "We are faced again with double loyalties and overlapping realms of power—international communism [read Islamic fundamentalism today] versus nation-state, transnational affinity versus nationalism—as well as with wars like those . . . in Korea and Indo-China that partake of the character of international and civil war simultaneously." If Wolfers is right, the cleavage between the older and the new patterns of international politics and between political and international theory may be diminished through what he describes as the "new medievalism."

The revitalization of political theory for international relations coincides with the end of the European age of international politics. Wolfers maintains that the "entry of the United States and other non-European countries as actors into the company of the world's leading powers . . . made past [international] theory . . . directly relevant to the United States as it was all along to the European nations to whom it was originally addressed." However, Wolfers draws a sharp distinction between European and Anglo-American approaches to international theory. He finds the source of the difference in what he calls "insular security." Continental theory centered on the idea of "necessity of state," which was the core of Machiavelli's perspective.[9] For Europeans geographical location and the nature of power subjected them to forces that were often beyond their control. They confronted a dilemma of reconciling the seemingly irreconcilable demands of necessity and the rule of law.

By contrast, English and American thinkers were soon caught up in a debate over the ideally best way of applying principles of morality to foreign policy. The Anglo-American philosophy was a philosophy of choice as against the European philosophy of necessity. Each philosophy was imperiled by certain dangers brought about by man's tendency toward excess: "The philosophy

9. *Ibid.*, xviii.

of necessity tends to lead to resignation, irresponsibility or even the glorification of amorality, [whereas] the philosophy of choice lends itself to excessive moralism and self-righteousness."[10] Notwithstanding, English and American theorists such as More, Bolingbroke, and Jefferson understood the advantages of an insular location. At times it enabled them to remain aloof and at other times free themselves through ideological rationalization from the taint of power politics. For them external attack or foreign invasion was an unlikely contingency. With all the differences between Locke and Jefferson, on one hand, and Hobbes, Hamilton, Bolingbroke, and Alfred Mahan on the other, the insular factor influenced the thinking of all of them.

Wolfers concludes that international theory is the product of "a single persistent historical situation extending back over more than four centuries." Those who write about theory for this period must be considered "contemporaries." Wolfers and Wight agree that international theory has not evolved in the direction of "solutions of ever greater perfection." In the growth of international thought there is "little accumulation of knowledge" or increasing depth of "insight" of the kind that characterizes other parts of "political knowledge."[11] If Hume's discussion of the balance of power had been written two centuries later its subject matter would be much the same as at the time it was actually written. Therefore, we legitimately return to and almost always learn from international theorists of the past. Translating "kings and subjects" to "decision makers and the public" brings past and present on line.

After World War II we confronted a significant change in the narrowing of possible areas of choice even for insular peoples. In the postwar era, they have for all practical purposes become Continental measured by the dangers and compulsions with which they are confronted. The question is how Anglo-American theorists and practitioners will respond. Wolfers warns against two immensely tempting but equally questionable responses. The one is to say with the Continentals that all decisions are dictated wholly by external circumstances. The other is to be oblivious to the sharp narrowing of the margins of choice for Anglo-Americans

10. *Ibid.,* xxi.
11. *Ibid.,* ix, xiii, xvi, xviii, xxi, xxv.

and to maintain that what is considered evil when undertaken by others is almost always seen as virtuous when carried out by oneself. It would be rank hypocrisy to suppose that participating in wars in remote places or threatening the use of force against weak neighbors or forming more and more alliances is cynically amoral for others but not for one's own self-righteous nation. Cynicism and hypocrisy are the twin dangers, both being expressions of humanity's excess, to which Wolfers makes repeated reference.

The third viewpoint maintains that certain concepts and problems such as authority, justice, power, and community which were present in ancient political systems are also present in contemporary international relations. We find a clear expression of this view in the continuing relevance of classical political theory. It may not be possible to find analogies with current international problems in every case, nor can it be shown that concepts apply equally in classical and contemporary societies. What the consideration of authority or justice or concepts of man and the state by classical writers facilitates is more careful and discriminating reflection on politics and international thought today. In perusing the Platonic dialogues, the reader or student achieves greater enlightenment on the issues that persist down to the present. And even when we reach no more than a few tentative conclusions, we advance in wisdom and understanding.

Two

Classical Political Thought

In turning to examine the classical tradition in political thought, the first question is, Where are we to look for points of convergence, if not congruence, between political theory and international thought? For some influential international theorists, such as Martin Wight, the contrasts are more numerous than the similarities. To be sure, international theory is less susceptible of the type of progressivist interpretation associated with the growth of nations. Political theory marches forward in continuous contact with political activity. The substance of political theory and political practice includes John Locke and the Glorious Revolution, Jeremy Bentham and administrative and prison reforms, and change from authoritarianism and absolutism to constitutional government and democracy.

Among the most significant achievements of national societies is the institutionalization of national unity through constitutional principles and historical development. Through the building of community, nations harmonize the forces of diversity. By contrast, international society is characterized by recurrent disharmony. Positive change based on shifting historical circumstances is more dramatically visible within individual sovereign states. It is striking, even in the 1990s, that dramatic political changes in the world came first within individual countries, as in such countries as Poland and Hungary in Eastern Europe, not in a brave new world order or in the early realization of transforming unity within a region. Moreover, the situation within each individual country reflects differing degrees of political, social, and economic change from Poland and Hungary to Romania and Bulgaria. Similarly, technological changes that have the capacity to transform domestic societies, as in nineteenth-century Russia, have more limited effects on the historic requirements for international stability such as alliances or the balance of power. In a word, change domestically is more dramatic than change in international relations.

Not only do such differences persist, but the limits on international theory are further manifest within three broad areas. Past and present political circumstances have influenced the character of international thought. First, relations among nations were viewed as unchanging until the nineteenth century and the ending of the Napoleonic Wars. Throughout the Middle Ages, war and strife were accepted as a fact of nature beyond the power of man to change or transform. Within societies, a similar attitude found expression in the acceptance of the inevitability of poverty and social class. The Enlightenment and reformist nationalism combined to modify such thinking. Enlightenment thinkers concluded that a new order was possible in which war and poverty would be eradicated. Second, theory in the late nineteenth and early twentieth centuries, as Wolfers and others demonstrate, focused on "what ought to be," not "what is." Wilsonianism did little to explore the connection between the "is" and the "ought." Other forces were at work that discredited idealism. With the rise of totalitarianism and fascism, disillusionment set in. Third, students and observers came to hold increasingly more modest expectations of international theory as a result of the complex relationship between recurrent and unique events in history—between historical experiences that repeat themselves and those that happen only once. As for providing guides to action, the most international theory appeared able to do was to point to alternative courses of action that might be possible under particular sets of circumstances. Theory in this sense can identify contingent factors, such as the effects of weather on military campaigns, a problem that persists even in high-tech confrontations like the Gulf War, or accidental and contingent realities such as the oft-cited example of the relation of Cleopatra's nose to the course of history. The limits on international theory are greater than the limits on political theory. The unknowns are more numerous and accidents more frequent. Certainty escapes political observers and leads some to question whether there can indeed be any international theory.

What, then, can international theory as such provide? Among the answers theorists have given is that it can bring order and meaning to otherwise-disparate bodies of information. As we struggle to understand the meaning of unrelenting conflict, such as warfare in the Persian Gulf or ethnic conflict in the former Eastern-bloc nations, theory can help us order the vast array of information the mass media brings into our homes. It can produce new knowledge by virtue of the questions it asks. The practical function of any theory depends on the political environment within which it operates. The more resistant that environment is to universalizing the precepts of political or military action, the greater the limits imposed on theory. The appearance of a Hitler or a Saddam Hussein sets limits on what can be said about recurrence and repetition in international society. Hence international theory sometimes can do no more than seek recourse to rough axioms such as those expressed by Hobbes—"nations are gladiators facing one another"—or Hamilton—"harmony is impossible among unconnected sovereignties"—or Bolingbroke—"self-love is the determining principle of international relations." Such axioms, incomplete as they may be, trace in rough measure some of the boundaries of politics on the international scene.

Political Discourse: Past and Present

Political theory seems to be far removed from many of the troublesome issues that characterize international theory. Not only is political theory addressed to the quest for objective truth and universals about man and politics, but the classical thinkers, whose work is a starting point in political theory, wrote more than 2,500 years ago about political societies bearing little resemblance to the mass societies of the late twentieth century. Today there is evidence on every hand of science and technology changing the world. Scientists confronting new scientific and technical problems seldom think of returning to the Greeks and the Romans for illumination. Modern science has advanced far beyond classical scientific thought.

In politics, however, the striking fact about the history of political thought is the reemergence of certain perennial issues and recurrent problems. The essentials of social and political problems do not change throughout history. However much the language and landscape of politics are altered, certain issues present themselves again and again for evaluation and discourse. They include the main patterns of relationships between the individual and the state, legitimacy and authority, law and morality versus naked power, the connections between force and violence, revolution, the common good, the purpose of the state, governance and government, equality and class, wealth and power, justice, order, freedom, community, and society. None of these issues has been discovered or invented in the twentieth century. The ancient Greeks, the Indian political philosophers, and the prophets of the Old Testament confronted many of the same problems. They sought to understand politics and the preconditions of a just and orderly political society. Politics and science require different standards, paradigms, and perspectives and the invoking of different traditions from different historical epochs.

In reflecting on the essence of philosophy, Jakob Burckhardt wrote of returning to the one central and irreducible reality on which all else is based: man. How we are to think of man and human nature is the root question. One place to begin is with the classical canons of Greek political thought. Men discover themselves in the image they observe in the responses of others. Twentieth-century sociologists call it the "mirrored self." In another context: "Do you know," asks Emerson, "the secret of the true scholar? In every man there is something wherein I may learn of him; and in that I am his pupil." Human nature has changed very little since the time of the Greeks. Statements about man notable for their clarity and cogency are found in many traditions, but it is political man and things political that are at the heart of classical political philosophy. What, then, is political man, and what is meant by *political?* Leo Strauss wrote: "Before one can even think of attempting to understand the nature of political things, one must know political things. At least every sane adult possesses political knowledge to some degree. Everyone knows something of taxes, police, law, jails, war, peace, armistice. . . . Everyone knows that buying a shirt, as distinguished from casting a vote, is not in itself a political action."[1]

Strauss goes on to defend the superiority of the classical tradition "characterized by noble simplicity and quiet grandeur."[2] Classical thought had its birth at a moment when all political traditions were shaken and before a tradition of political philosophy existed. The Owl of Minerva, symbolizing wisdom, appears at the twilight of civilization. In later historical periods, men viewed politics as if through a screen of language and methodology separating the observer from political reality. Classical thought looks on political things with a directness and freshness that continues to be unequaled. Classical political philosophers do not look at political things from the outside, as spectators of political life. They speak the language of citizens or soldiers or statesmen: they hardly use a single term that is not familiar in the marketplace. Where citizens and political thinkers share common terms, however they may differ in the depth of their understanding, political discourse is possible about the state, society, and politics.

George H. Sabine begins his *History of Political Theory* with the words: "Most modern political ideals—such, for example, as justice, liberty, constitutional government and respect for the law—or at least the definitions of them, began with the reflection of Greek thinkers about the institution of the city-state."[3] The city-state was small in area and population. Athens was comparable with Denver or Rochester half a century ago. Its three main classes were slaves, resident foreigners, and the citizenry, entitled to take part in political life. Some, but not all, public business was conducted in the Assembly, or town meeting, which every Athenian was expected to attend when he reached twenty-five years of age. Political participation was the road to self-realization. For modern international relations, participation in international organizations sometimes has led to self-determination for nations, but for the Armenians and Serbs and the people of Croatia and Bosnia-Hercegovina this has hardly been the case. Politics for Athenians was everyone's business within the boundaries established for the

1. Leo Strauss, *What Is Political Philosophy?* (Glencoe, Ill., 1959), 14.
2. *Ibid.,* 28.
3. George H. Sabine, *A History of Political Theory* (New York, 1937), 3.

work of the Assembly. Effective control of government lay in the hands of representative groups such as the Council of Five Hundred and the courts with large popular juries.

In the early chapters of this study we shall seek areas in which we can find similarities between political theory and international relations theory. What are the themes that unite and those that divide the two spheres? What are their common concerns and their disparate interests? Can we point to overlapping interests, or are their paths always separate and distinct from each other? Which of the three interpretations we have considered best explains the relationship between political and international relations theory? What are the lessons to be drawn from the ancients, the fifteenth and sixteenth centuries, and the political thinkers of the seventeenth through nineteenth centuries? This is the inquiry on which we embark in a series of chapters on the great political thinkers who have dominated the history of political thought. The focus is on their relevance for international relations in the late twentieth and twenty-first centuries.

Three

Plato (427–347 B.C.)

Plato was the descendant of a prominent family in the Age of Pericles. Pericles is remembered as the author of the famous Funeral Oration in honor of soldiers who fell in the first year of the Peloponnesian war with Sparta. Even today historians describe Pericles' Oration as the finest statement of a political ideal in any language. It expresses the intimacy and nobility of life in the Greek city-state. Athens had found an answer to the dilemma of reconciling private and public life. As Pericles explains in the Oration: "We alone regard a man who takes no interest in public affairs, not as a harmless, but as a useless character; and if few of us are originators, we are all sound judges of policy." No man is born to office, and no man can buy office. Man achieves virtue within the state.

Through what Plato in *The Republic* was to criticize as "happy versatility," each man rises to the level to which his natural gifts entitle him. Pericles compared Athens with Sparta thus: "Whereas they from early youth are always undergoing laborious exercises which are to make them brave, we live at ease, and yet are equally ready to face the perils which they face." A twentieth-century parallel may be the Israeli army, some of whose soldiers are performing artists with symphony orchestras; when conflict breaks out, they exchange their musical instruments for rifles and go off to war. A parallel in our time would be young American students trading books for bayonets in World War II. Athenians were strong as amateurs are strong. They claim superiority, not from expert knowledge or highly trained specialization, but from intellectual virtuosity. However, in comparing various regimes Plato goes on to speak of "happy versatility" as the ineradicable defect of any democratic regime. In this, he anticipates the modern discussion of public service, including Thomas Jefferson's concept of an aristocracy of talents, Jacksonian populist democracy, and the idea of meritocracy. Thucydides wrote of the distance between the ideal state and its flawed reality in Athens, marred by excess, factionalism, and bitter rivalries among a citizenry whose vices did not stem from ignorance; on the contrary, they knew one another all too well. In Athens, "reckless daring . . . [became] loyal courage; prudent delay was the excuse of the coward; moderation was the disguise of unmanly weakness; to know everything was to do nothing. . . . The tie of party was stronger than the tie of blood."[1] The ideal and reality were separated in practice as was to be the case throughout political history.

Plato from age eighteen to age twenty-one was a devoted companion and pupil of Socrates. Shocked by the trial and death of Socrates for corrupting youth and denying the gods, he left Athens for the city of Megara, then traveled throughout Italy, Sicily, and Egypt before returning to Athens to found the first so-called European university, the Academy. He lectured on philosophy and mathematics but also on aspects of politics, despite his disillusionment with the conduct of the state after the death of Socrates. In 367 B.C., at age sixty, he seized the opportunity to educate a contemporary prince, Dionysius II of Syracuse (sometimes called Dion), in the precepts of the philosopher-king. Wearying of his exacting studies and personal jealousies, the prince left Plato, who returned to the Academy and resumed his teaching. Twenty years later he died, ten years before Philip of Macedon secured hegemony over the whole of the Greek world.

The Platonic dialogues take up Socrates' quest for truth and, in the words of some commentators, improve on it. Plato speaks of Socrates as being "rejuvenated and beautified" through political discourse. Nothing is settled in the dialogues, yet everything is somehow clarified and illuminated. Philosophy for Plato and Socrates is love of the quest for wisdom rather than the pronounce-

1. Thucydides, *History of the Peloponnesian War,* trans. Rex Warner (Harmondsworth, Eng., 1954), Bk. III.

ment of truth. Plato's world is a world of ideals and values, but, in John Dewey's phrase, it is also "a realm of things with all their imperfections removed." In a feigned spirit of ignorance Socrates questions, not as the Sophists did, leading their students toward some desired end, but in an effort to gain a fuller understanding of the essence or the essential form and character of an idea or a virtue. Socrates' method is dialectical, the tracing of an idea to its underlying postulate. For example, he asks on what premise or assumption the idea of security rests, or equality, or justice. He searches for examples that will explain and illuminate the principle.

For Plato, wisdom is the essential virtue of which all other virtues are but examples or limited expressions. As Socrates had defined the cardinal virtues, courage is fearlessness before objects that wisdom shows are not to be feared. It is more than "reckless daring." Temperance is the *appropriate* restraint of bodily passions. For Socrates wisdom is the one good thing, stupidity or dullness the one bad thing. Men seek wisdom in discourse, not in wealth or power or popularity or polls. Plato's ideas are the universals that Socrates was forever pursuing. Ideas are the shadows the sun throws on the wall of the cave, which men perceive dimly but which can guide them toward the truth. It may be instructive to ask how Plato's conception of the ideal (the *idos*) can be compared with Woodrow Wilson's version of the ideal.

The two works that critics and commentators identify with Plato's politics are *The Republic* and *The Laws*. *The Republic,* described by some as Plato's central work, is an inquiry into justice, the just man, and the just state. It is *not* primarily an inquiry into just war, a topic that preoccupies certain international relations theorists. Justice for the individual is that kind of life in which "every part of the soul" fulfills its intended role: it is linked with the concept of proportion. Justice for the state involves each individual fulfilling his intended role and each class realizing its intended purpose. Critics and defenders alike speak of the Republic as the first utopia, the first heavenly city, the perfect city in the sky. Beholding it, men undertake to make their own cities more perfect, yet for Plato the two cities are separated forever. It is a city whose foundations rest on philosophical speculation, not social engineering.

Large segments of *The Republic* treat the nature of philosophy and more particularly the education of the philosopher. Sentences appear that provoke controversy and generate continuing debate, such as, "Cities will not cease from evil until kings are philosophers or philosophers are kings." Karl Popper and other critics ask, "What happens to democracy and the 'open society' when philosophers are kings?" Is Platonism fundamentally antidemocratic? Reinhold Niebuhr would observe that philosophers no less than other mortals are prone to do evil. Apologists respond that *The Republic* is not a book on politics but a book on morals. Philosophers will not become kings nor kings philosophers except in the perfect city in the sky, which is not now and never will be a city of this world. (*Utopia* translates as "no place.")

To those who complain that Plato's state is authoritarian or despotic, Plato would respond that what he seeks is order in a world of chaos. He saw chaos as the great corruption of his times. Plato is not proposing an ideal commonwealth or transformation of the structure of government. Yet his ideal is the real state. Any state that falls short is not completely a state. Man must look at the city that is within his soul and "take heed that no disorder occurs." The ethical, not the political, aspect of the theory is attainable. In Glaucon's words, "In heaven there is laid up a pattern . . . which he who desires may behold, and beholding may set his house in order." It matters not whether such a pattern exists or ever will exist. The wise man will follow the ways of that city and have nothing to do with any other.[2]

Philosophers and rulers are, of course, not the whole of society. Warriors, also known as guardians (soldiers in wartime, armed auxiliaries in peace), and loyal administrators also serve society. Each has his own peculiar virtue—for example, philosophers wisdom and guardians courage. Each does for the state what certain virtues do for the individual. Warriors are to the state what courage, loyalty, and enlightened passion are to the individual. The worker class, which participates in the physical and industrial activities of the state, aspires to temperance and discipline. If all classes perform in accordance with their intended virtues, justice will prevail in the state. The order of *The Republic* throughout is architectonic and hierarchical. The aim of the state is not to make citizens happy but to make the state and the individual just even if

2. Plato, *The Republic,* ed. Charles M. Bakewell (New York, 1928), xlii.

this goal requires purifying the themes of political discourse and preventing poets and musicians from arousing the emotions of men. All this is heresy for freedom-loving people and societies until we reflect on such novel contemporary restraints as laws about drugs, bans on alcohol at fraternity parties, checkpoints for drunken drivers, restrictions on beer ads, and baggage searches at airports. Even present-day disputes over public funding of the arts are directed at certain kinds of music and art rather than art in general.

What, then, is to be the education of the philosopher? How are a select group of youths to advance toward wisdom and virtue? Plato answers that they must be helped to move from things temporal to an awareness of eternal truths. Education of the philosopher must turn "the eye of the soul" from the shadows on the cave wall to certain unchanging realities. Mathematics or form and numbers are the first stage in the educational process and dialectics the final phase. Having undertaken many moral and intellectual disciplines, philosophic candidates return at age thirty-five to the "cave" of the world, where for fifteen years they test their "principles" and determine whether they "will stand firm or flinch." At age fifty they "come at last to their consummation. . . . they must raise the eye of the soul to the universal light . . . for that is the pattern according to which they are to order the state and their own lives also, making philosophy their chief pursuit but when their time comes, toiling also at politics and ruling for the public good." A sound polity is dependent on the sound education of its rulers. In the 1950s and 1960s, I remember Harvard's Carl J. Friedrich applying this principle literally to his contemporaries when he argued that no one could become a philosopher before age fifty.

To some of the aforementioned views of Plato, Leo Strauss offered his own independent interpretation. Not *The Republic* but *The Laws,* according to Strauss, is Plato's political work par excellence. *The Laws* is a conversation about law and politics between an old Athenian stranger, an old Cretan, and an old Spartan on the island of Crete. The Athenian has come in search of the best ancestral laws, which presumably are Cretan. Why are they best? The answer is that they were god-given through Zeus instructing his son Minos, the Cretan legislator. Who says they are god-given? It turns out only the poet Homer says so, and poets, we are told, are of questionable veracity. The discussion shifts back and forth to whether Crete's laws are intrinsically good or whether Athenian laws are better. After a long, rambling exchange on wine drinking and homosexuality practiced within Athens and Crete and relating to their laws, the discussion turns to the question of the best regime. The character of the governing body and of the legislator is determined by the regime, and regime is the order that gives society its character. Strauss writes: "Regime is the form of life as living together, the manner of living in society. . . . Regime means the whole, which we today are in the habit of viewing primarily in a fragmentized form: regime means simultaneously the form of life of a society . . . its moral taste, form of society, form of state, form of government, spirit of laws."[3] It is fair to ask whether regime theory in international relations in the 1990s can approach the coherence and comprehensiveness of Plato's thought. Or is it but a pale and incomplete version of Plato's "regime"? Expressed in the context of *politics,* political life is activity directed toward a goal. To pursue such a goal society must be constituted and organized in accordance with that goal. A good regime will in general reflect a worthy goal.

For international relations, the twin ideas that derive from Plato's discussion of regime are, first, the interrelation of regimes (inter-regime relations) and, second, the question that preoccupies classical political philosophy, that of the best regime. Strauss asserts that "each regime raises a claim, explicitly or implicitly, which extends beyond the boundaries of any given society. These claims conflict . . . therefore with each other." They demand that mankind decide which of the regimes is best. Is this definition an anticipation of mid-twentieth-century ideological warfare or competitive coexistence? Plato cautions that even under favorable circumstances, the realization of the best regime rests on contingencies no one can foresee. "The actualization of the best regime depends on the coming together . . . of things which have a natural tendency to move away from each other (e.g., on the coincidence or conflict of philosophy and political power); its actualization depends therefore on chance."[4] The coming together of philosophy

3. Leo Strauss, *What Is Political Philosophy?* (Glencoe, Ill., 1959), 34.
4. *Ibid.*

and power is a near miracle because of the dual nature of man, who is an in-between being (*metaxis*) living a life somewhere between that of a brute and a god.

The lessons to be derived for international theory are less explicit and direct than with Augustine or Machiavelli, both of whom speak in concrete terms of war and international systems. We are tempted to conclude that Martin Wight was right in arguing that political theory takes as its subject the state and not semianarchic interstate relations. Yet certain propositions in Plato prefigure some of the great debates in international relations and are worthy of attention in this chapter.

The first concerns the nature of morality within and between states. The title of Niebuhr's much-discussed volume *Moral Man and Immoral Society* speaks for an important body of present-day thought. According to realist thought, the highest moral end for the ruler is preserving the state; by contrast, the individual may try to live in accordance with the Sermon on the Mount. The individual may sacrifice himself for a purpose that transcends self-interest, whereas the responsible ruler is duty bound to safeguard the state. Therefore, Niebuhr distinguishes between two types of morality. By contrast, Plato considers public and private morality as being identical. The school of justice is the same for the private person in his relationships as it is for the ruler of the city. In Book IV of *The Republic,* Socrates maintains that "wisdom is the same in the man and in the city. Courage in the city is the same as courage in the individual. Virtue is the same quality in both. A man and a city will be deemed just or unjust according to the same standards."[5] There are standards and objective truth beyond history by which both private and public norms are judged even as the American higher law tradition is the basis of the first ten amendments to the Constitution.

A second issue raised in *The Dialogues* concerns attitudes toward war and heroes. Socrates questions the validity of some of the virtues attributed to the gods by saying that the gods, Homer notwithstanding, plainly have feet of clay. Their vices exceed those of ordinary mortals and offer weak examples for the guidance of mankind on earth. In this connection, it is worth remembering

5. Plato, *The Republic,* trans. Richard W. Sterling and William C. Scott (New York, 1985), Bk. IV, l. 135.

that Socrates taught not by invoking authority but by the more negative process of leading men to see the fallacy of their beliefs. He pointed the way to good government and good education by showing the ways in which Greek democracy suffered from class war, bad government, and bad education.

Third, Plato through Socrates set forth certain principles of war and the causes of war. Having discussed the wants of artisans, merchants, and sailors, Plato shows how their desires multiply, not only for food or sofas or tables but for "dainties and perfumes" and "incense and cakes." As people seek more than necessities they enlarge their borders. They need more servants, tutors, and contractors, and the country that offers enough to support the original inhabitants becomes too small. Socrates continues: "Then a slice of our neighbor's land will be wanted . . . and they will want a slice of ours, if, like ourselves, they exceed the limits of necessity and give themselves up to the unlimited accumulation of wealth." He concludes: "And so we shall go to war, Glaucon." The process continues and "our State must once more enlarge; and this time the enlargement will be nothing short of a whole army, which will have to go out and fight . . . for all that we have."[6] Plato's theory of war is that a state seeks more territory in response to the growing needs and acquisitiveness of its people.

Some contemporary theorists would view this as an economic theory of war. If so, how would Plato account for wars with political and territorial rather than economic objectives? It is clear that Plato does not glorify war, for he sees it as deriving from "causes which are also the causes of almost all the evils in states, private as well as public." Yet war is an art, and like the tasks of a shoemaker or a weaver or a builder no man "who takes up a shield or other implement of war [can] become a good fighter all in a day."[7] Hence war is the responsibility of the few and not the many, who lack both the spirit and the specialized training. It is the task of a small, well-trained professional body rather than the mass of citizenry. From the time of the French Revolution, the movement of mobilizing armies has shifted from the direction Plato prescribed.

As we look back on Plato's thought, it is striking how many of

6. Plato, *The Republic,* ed. Bakewell, 70–71.
7. *Ibid.*, 72.

the issues with which moderns contend are foreshadowed. His unceasing quest for wisdom rather than the everlasting pronouncement of "truth" has relevance for the television age. The electronic media and the style of editorialists echo with self-righteousness, and some columnists and broadcast evangelists apparently see themselves as speaking words of absolute truth. It may be that the Socratic dialogue is ill adapted to mass societies. Using the dialectic method, Socrates struggled to discover the underlying assumptions on which prevailing ideas are based. The dialogues never settle once and for all the questions over which philosophers and the citizenry contend. They do not offer many final answers. They do clarify and illuminate and bring men closer to wisdom.

So it is with many of the other contentious issues that moderns face. Plato discusses the question of whether private and public morality are the same, and while his answers may not satisfy some modern thinkers, they pose problems that must be confronted once again today. Plato considers the questions surrounding debates over the nature of man and political man. While pursuing the goals of a political philosopher and political thinker, he discusses the limits of theory, which fails to take account of the multitude of contingencies and accidents that shape history. In relation to theory, the language of politics is a key issue. The figures in Plato's dialogues speak in the language of citizens and soldiers. No one group has a monopoly on recasting the language of politics, although some political scientists have tried (Harold Lasswell). Some present-day theories are too narrow in scope compared, say, with Plato's reference to the entire society as a regime. Debates over the issue of a career service in government continue, and Plato, drawing on Pericles' Funeral Oration, examines the myriad factors that have to be considered. War and heroes and the causes of war and conditions of peace are taken up, as are all the questions regarding the best regime. For many contemporaries the issue of the best regime is a nonquestion, for they assert unequivocally the supremacy of democracy beyond all other regimes. Students of Plato ask whether democracy is appropriate for every culture. Plato also has a philosophy of education. His idea of justice and equality rests on ideas that throw shadows on the wall of a cave. Policies are judged by transcendent standards rather than by purposes that find their meaning wholly within history. Justice means every individual must realize his intended purpose within history, as must every class. These and other aspects of Plato's philosophy suggest that he was more than a philosopher; he was a philosopher of interstate relations whose intellectual agenda included the great perennial issues such as justice and, further, whose approach has merit today as we reflect on democracy and the best regime, war and peace, morality within and among states, political or practical wisdom, freedom and order, and the interrelation of laws and regimes.

Four

Aristotle (384–322 B.C.)

Aristotle, who was Plato's greatest student, was born not in Athens but in Stagira, Thrace, a frontier outpost of Greek settlements. As with many foreign-born in a country not of their birth, Aristotle exhibited an intense patriotism. We remember that Napoleon was a Corsican.

Aristotle inherited an abiding respect for science from his father, a physician who became court physician in Pella, the Macedonian capital not far from Albania and the troubled area of Kosova. At age eighteen, Aristotle was drawn to Athens and Plato's Academy, where he remained for the next twenty years. He was to Plato what Nehru was to Gandhi, his most outstanding yet independent-minded disciple. With Plato's death in 347 B.C., Aristotle left Athens and in 343 became the teacher of Alexander of Macedon, who was on the threshold of one of history's most far-reaching conquests, leading to an expanding empire throughout Asia and most of the known world. Aristotle's emphasis on limits, moderation, and restraint—what came to be called the Golden Mean—was antithetical to Alexander's exuberance, expansiveness, and excesses. The triumphalism of a recently elected president or of a conqueror on the march often blinds him to the need for moderation, or for what Dean Rusk once described as consultation with a "wait-a-minute man." Ironically, Aristotle looked down on the Asians that Alexander conquered as the lowest of all barbarians, while Alexander sought to give the conquered people a stake in the empire. Does this suggest that rulers are sometimes more in touch with the potentialities of the common man than intellectuals preoccupied with their own theories? Or was Aristotle led to criticize Asians for other reasons?

Aristotle returned to Athens, where he founded his own school, the Lyceum. During the next twelve years he taught students and directed a constitutional history of 158 Greek cities. Whereas Plato was the idealist, Aristotle was the empiricist. Despite his break with Alexander, Aristotle felt that, like Socrates, his position was endangered in Athens. He escaped the anti-Macedonian demonstrations after Alexander's death by fleeing to Euboea, where he died in 322 a sickly, thin-legged, and balding little man with few remaining ties to Greece.

Aristotle's major works are apparently fragments of writings used in teaching but not prepared for publication. His greatest work, *Politics,* cannot be considered a finished book such as he might have written for a wider public. It is, in effect, a collection of chapters and essays. Books II, III, VII, and VIII concern the ideal state and were written soon after Plato's death, using his philosophy as a jumping-off point. Books IV, V, and VI provide a comparative analysis of actual state forms in various stages of development and decay. Book I was probably written last and is imperfectly joined to Book II. It reflects Aristotle's approach to actual forms of government, underlying social forces, and the instruments of statecraft.

Aristotle's discourse is deceptively simple. It has the ring of plain common sense. A more careful reading produces new understandings, and every time one reads him one finds something new. In much the way that Aristotle must be read with reference to Plato, both of them must be seen in relation to the Sophists, who were the dominant school of the day. They were the respectable school to whom the better classes in Athens sent their children to study rhetoric and other subjects. The Sophists were "the establishment," and for contemporaries the term had positive connotations. *Sophism* comes from *Sophia,* which means "wisdom." Yet the Sophists marketed themselves as willing and able to teach the young the skill of justifying in rhetoric any point of view or its opposite. Plato and Aristotle set out to demolish the Sophists' totally relativistic viewpoint. Sophism is represented in Plato's *Republic* by Thrasymachus, who says that justice in society is always the right of the stronger. (We shall see that Thucydides makes a comparable claim in the Melian dialogue not for society in general but as between two warring states in an anarchic interstate society.) To this day, controversy surrounds discussion of morality and power and objective versus relativist standards or norms.

In *Politics* and his discussion of different states and constitutions, Aristotle argues that "statesmen must consider not only the absolute best conditions." The best government may be a mixture of the actual and the ideal. This is the essence of success in forming a government and writing a constitution. The way to think about constitutions is to reflect on the conditions of a people and the constitution they require. The English and their common law tradition may be best served by an unwritten constitution, the Americans by a written one, and the Israelis by no constitution at all. Constitutions should reflect the political genius, habits, and mode of a people. In certain countries—the Weimar Republic, Republican Spain, and pre-1989 Eastern Europe—democratic constitutions have actually undermined democracy. Six volumes published by the Miller Center at the University of Virginia explore constitutionalism in Africa, Asia, Latin America, and Europe, including Eastern Europe. In every case, it was found that constitutions that survive take root in the culture of a society and the customs of its people.

Aristotle's most famous classification in *Politics* divides states into monarchy, aristocracy, and polity. Each has its own peculiar corruption—tyranny, oligarchy, and democracy, respectively. There are many kinds of democracy: middle-class, agrarian, and proletarian among others. Aristotle says each is known for its own partial conception of justice rather than its realization of absolute justice. In practice, legislative compromises among groups come closer to justice than ideological dogma. Aristotle appears to be anticipating the current debate over absolute and relative justice and the extension of democracy around the world.

To be healthy, the state must have a proper distribution of power between those best qualified to govern and those who constitute the mass of the citizenry. A balance needs to be struck between qualitative and quantitative principles. A society that tends too much toward aristocracy should have its democratic elements strengthened and vice versa. The best government is one in which a strong middle class predominates because it makes possible Aristotle's polity, or limited government. Seemingly by instinct, the electorate in the United States has some comprehension of this principle.

What is the contemporary relevance of these propositions more broadly conceived? Extrapolating from Aristotle's ideas, we know that the U.S. Constitution limits the power of the masses in two ways. The first is by providing different electorates and times of election for the House, Senate, and president, including indirect election of the president. The second is by requiring judicial review. Jefferson wanted control by a large middle class of farmers and mechanics each of whom owned his own means of production; Aristotle speaks of property giving the citizenry a true stake in their government. In every country, at some time, the lines have been drawn between those for whom property or the means of production count and those lacking property and therefore denied the franchise at least for a time.

Vast concentrations of economic, financial, and technological power in the twentieth century raise questions concerning the distribution of power in present-day society. An institution may appear to be democratic on its face but be undemocratic in practice, for example, a plebiscitarian democracy, whose advocates make claims of speaking for all the people much as tyrants invoked religion in an earlier day. Plebiscitarianism in varying degrees characterized the regimes of Napoleon I, Napoleon III, Hitler, and Stalin—and today Saddam Hussein. Plebiscites display all the paraphernalia of democracy, including free elections, but actually lack true freedom of choice among legitimate alternatives. Or, in what Aristotle called slum democracies, voters are excluded by literacy tests and other disqualifying requirements. Aristocrats and totalitarian rulers often act in today's world in the name of democracy.

Aristotle also discusses equality and in effect asks, "Equal in relation to what?" His answer is that men are equal in relation to their capacity to govern. However, classical thought assumes some men are better qualified than others for any given profession. Yet critics ask, What happens if society establishes criteria for governing that exclude a prepresidential Lincoln or Truman? And if some are better suited to govern, what happens to the equality of those they govern? If society determines that one man or a small group is politically superior and therefore deserving to rule, does this approach not destroy political equality? What about the corrupting influence of power among rulers? The Greeks had an institution to check such influence, and they called it *ostracism*. Its purpose was to re-create conditions of equality between the rulers and the ruled. It was intended to remove those who had grown too powerful and judged themselves to be above the law or the constitution.

In one place Aristotle says that certain charismatic rulers are like gods and therefore the rules do not apply to them. In another place he states that an enduring requirement of political equality is that government must be limited, as with a constitutional government. Americans speak of checks and balances. No one, however wise or virtuous, is beyond subjecting himself to political competition. When we speak of equality, we come face to face with an insoluble antinomy, a combination of opposites. Whenever one person rules over another person, he imposes his will on the other—a paradigm of inequality. Truly, a just political order is based on the principle of equality, but it is in the nature of politics to divide men on the basis of inequality. Rulers "lord it over others." The best practical and attainable goal, therefore, is an accommodation, or *modus vivendi,* or some kind of compromise between these antinomies. The essence of politics requires some form of organic relation between political power, political freedom, and political equality.

Aristotle holds to the concept of the virtue of the good man. Both Aristotle and Plato were in search of an objective distinction between opinion and truth. Plato found it in the *idos,* the ideal or the essence of things, which represents the true reality beyond the reality we perceive with our senses. Aristotle introduces the concept of the *telos,* or the innate purpose that exists for every living thing. The acorn achieves its realization and purpose when it becomes an oak. In every living being, in men and beasts, a teleological principle exists in which the *telos* is fulfilled. Aristotle asks, "What then is the *telos* of man?" How does man achieve the purpose for which he exists?

Aristotle answers in the first sentence of *Politics:* "Every state is a community of some kind and every community is established with a view to some good. The state or the political community is man's highest community and embraces all other communities." The *telos* of the family is the physical survival of its members, but the *telos* of the state is to provide the good life. The good man realizes himself in citizenship and in the perfection of qualities necessary for citizenship.

Aristotle points up the difference between the good citizen and the good man. The former seeks a kind of functional goodness. The good citizen achieves those virtues that are essential to the governance of the state in much the same way that the warrior attains the virtues necessary to the defense of the state. The good man realizes the virtues that are essential to the ideal state. His virtue goes beyond the narrower functional virtues that are necessary to be a good citizen or a good warrior. The good man realizes himself in the fullness of virtue and the good. The virtue of the good citizen cannot match the broad moral vision of the good man. Only in the ideal state are the two identical. The rulers of an imperfect state can only remain rulers by compromising the quest for full virtue. The ruled in the ideal state do not require the moral virtue of a good man even to fulfill their function as citizens. These distinctions give content to some of the differences between the good man and the good citizen.

Perhaps of all of Aristotle's political philosophy the core idea is justice, and justice is the core of contemporary political discourse. Whether the question has to do with the merits of a political system or institutional arrangements or political actions, the issue is justice. The standard of evaluation that is applied, whether explicitly or implicitly, is justice. Oligarchy is the rule of the wealthy, and the standard here is the possession of wealth. The wealthy enjoy more rights and benefits from the state. In democracy, the principle of justice is the exact opposite: all those of equal birth and born free have equal rights. In democracy, the principle of justice is equated with the principle of equality. Here Aristotle and modern thought are one.

If justice in democracy can be equated with equality, the question arises, "Equal with regard to what?" Oligarchy assumes that those who are equal in wealth should be treated equally. Democracy posits equality for all those who are free-born citizens. Yet empirically, with reference to the activities and qualities relevant to social life, all men are not equal. Those who contribute most to the true end (*telos*) of the state should be treated unequally. Those who are equal are those who contribute equally to the public good. In other words, those who are equal in the respects that are most relevant to the common good and the state should be dealt with equally. But how is this principle to be applied in practice? How do we determine who contributes most to the common good? The wealthy pay the highest taxes. Sometimes the poor pay no taxes at all. However, economic contributions are only one among many types of contributions the individual can make to the common good. What about public service or membership in the Peace Corps or service on the school board or in the civil service or the armed forces?

The lack of an objective standard for evaluating and comparing contributions to the common good is further complicated by two prevailing views of democracy in the United States. One is the principle embodied in *Federalist* 51, which has been used to justify pluralism in politics. According to this view, no objective principle exists for determining justice in democracy. The principle of justice therefore tends to be equated with success. Who gets what, where, and when determines justice. Where contradictory interests and pressure groups are involved, conflict becomes inevitable and is more likely to be resolved, not by the invoking of some objective standard of justice, but by the distribution of power between the contending groups.

The opposite concept of justice within democracy is inherent in the existence of a higher or transcendent standard. Americans refer to such a standard as the higher law tradition. The famous debates between Stephen Douglas and Abraham Lincoln found both leaders invoking the Declaration of Independence with its assertion that all men are created equal to justify their interpretation of slavery. Douglas maintained the Declaration applied to white men, or those descended from the British. Lincoln held that the Declaration applied to all men regardless of color or ancestors. If the principle of equality were limited to white men descended from the British, half of the American population in 1858 would have been excluded, Lincoln argued.

Politics in democracy is indeed a matter of interests and power, but it also assumes a moral framework, whether in law or in morality. Aristotle appears to assign higher standing to the polity (and its corruption, democracy) than to aristocracy. Three citizens consulting and acting together may attain a higher degree of justice than one man acting alone. While Aristotle recognizes the inevitability of the contest for influence in politics, classical thought views politics as subsumed in ethics. It is worth noting that Aristotle's optimism about the virtue of the individual citizen may reflect the limited size of Athens and other city-states and the minority who held the status of citizens. The founding fathers were skeptical about the wisdom and virtue of mass populations, and this attitude even then was a result of the character of the crowd. (Hamilton referred to the people as "the great beast.")

In conclusion, Aristotle's great contribution was in anticipating many of the issues of democracy that have been debated over the past two millennia. He also helps us understand the difference between the philosopher and the ruler. As the teacher of Alexander of Macedon, Aristotle taught limits, moderation, and restraint—and ultimately balance. Alexander exemplified expansiveness, excess, and exuberance. These different qualities distinguished the philosopher from the military and political leader. On justice, Aristotle sought to distinguish between Thrasymachus' concept of justice being the right of the stronger and power being subordinate to morality.

In the democratic era, when the goal of the United States is to export democracy to the world, Aristotle's approach to the question of the best regime has relevance. Without offering an answer to the question of whether democracy will be the best regime for years into the future, Aristotle's list of the better regimes (monarchy, aristocracy, and polity) and the corrupted and corruptible regimes (tyranny, oligarchy, and democracy) offers food for thought. In the discussion, Aristotle helps the reader to think again about the strengths and limitations of various forms of governance, including democracy. He warns about regimes that have all the trappings of democracy without its essence.

Finally, Aristotle's discussion of the state challenges us to rethink some modern ideas about the state. For Aristotle the state is man's highest community, embracing all the others. His conception of the state includes more than the system of governance. The problem Americans have is that a segment of the population sees no virtue at all in the state. It may be that the negative feelings we have about presidents and Congress go back to negative feelings about the state. Without in any way favoring the totalitarian state, we may wish to consider whether the low esteem in which many hold the state may be due not just to lapses in Congress but also to a more general downgrading of the state.

Five

Augustine (A.D. 354–430)

Augustine, bishop of Hippo in Africa, is considered by many the greatest political thinker in the era from Aristotle to Aquinas. For some he is the bridge between classical and modern thought, for others the first philosopher of history, and for everyone the first major thinker to develop a general analysis of the Christian philosophy of society and politics. At the same time, it must be acknowledged that Augustine was not a systematic thinker. He produced no *Summa Theologica* as did Aquinas, no single authoritative, comprehensive work with which he can be associated. His discussion of human nature, law, justice, moral obligation, and evil hardly constitutes a particularly orderly or coherent presentation. However, he is often called the first political realist because of his emphasis on human limitations, and therein lies his relevance for contemporary international relations.

Augustine's two most important books are *The Confessions,* written from 397 to 401 as he matured in years from forty-three to forty-seven, and *The City of God,* begun in 413 and completed in 425. The latter was a long, discursive work to which he devoted a full twelve years of his life, completing it when he was seventy-one. He also wrote other works, including *The Trinity, Commentaries on the Psalms, Commentaries on the Gospel and Epistles of St. John,* and occasional papers such as *Contra* (Against). He devoted much of his time and energy to disputations and rebuttals of the Donatist, Manichaean, and Pelagian heresies. He was a teacher of rhetoric and an ecclesiastical administrator with profound influence on the Roman Catholic church in Africa. He was a theologian and the author of a rule followed by many Catholic religious orders even today. His life was a parable of his times as he moved from adolescent sensualism to Manichaeanism to Neoplatonism, finally becoming ruling bishop of the church in Africa.

One parallel between Plato and Aristotle, on one hand, and Augustine, on the other, is that all three lived in times of dissolution of traditional institutions and beliefs. The crisis that Plato and Aristotle described was the crisis of the *polis,* or city-state, as well as the decline of the strongest military powers such as Sparta. The crisis in the city-state involved rifts and conflicts between the rich and poor, recurrent battles in the Peloponnesian War, and failure to create a larger political federation of states capable of solving society's most urgent problems. It is striking that many political philosophers whose writings are still read and discussed today wrote in times of trouble: Machiavelli in a period of instability during the Renaissance, Hobbes during conflict and civil war in seventeenth-century England, Rousseau at a moment of rising dissatisfaction with the ancien régime in France. The Owl of Minerva sounds as darkness descends over the land.

The age in which Augustine lived, the late fourth and early fifth centuries, was indeed a time of disintegration and change. It marked the transition between the classical civilizations of Greece and Rome and the medieval Christian civilization of western Europe. Heir to classical thought, Augustine was the father of Christian philosophy and theology. He sought to maintain traditional ideas while responding to a changing situation. Barbarians were moving into Europe and being Romanized through a system of Roman education and bureaucracy. Many were given or simply appropriated Roman titles and above all Roman citizenship. Despite these gestures of imperial acceptance and respect for a defeated enemy, Rome was profoundly shaken by the incursion of barbarians—Visigoths, Ostrogoths, and Vandals—overrunning Italy's heartland and culminating in the Sack of Rome by Alaric. Augustine was as shocked as his contemporaries, but when the otherworldliness of Christians was blamed for Rome's decline, he stirred himself to respond. Writing in *The City of God,* he argued that Rome's corruption and internal decay, rather than the weakening by Christianity of Roman resolve and imperial pride, led to Rome's downfall.

Even more than Spinoza, Augustine was a "God-intoxicated man." He maintained that the world was created by God. However, the City of Man was not eternal. It had had a beginning and would have an end, which would coincide with the Last Judgment. Man was created good but had lost his goodness and innocence with the Fall. He became a victim of self-pride. He had been created good in God's image but not incorruptibly good. He refused to accept his status as part creature by nature and came to see himself as wholly creator. According to Augustine, the root cause of sin is man's prideful self-centeredness. It is finite man refusing to accept his finiteness. Man seeks to make himself the lord of the universe. He seeks to dominate others and use them as means to his ends. Man's life is a restless and never-ending quest for power and for unremitting self-gratification with one conquest following another. For Augustine, original sin came into the world with the Fall, and through it the human race became "sick and sore . . . from Adam to the end of the world."

Yet God has not abandoned suffering humanity and never will. By means of unmerited grace, man is enabled to preserve some residual virtue. Through the Incarnation, God has given assurance that an elect group will receive salvation. Augustine insists that God is just in condemning the majority for Adam's sin. However, a few men such as Saul (who becomes Paul) will be saved "on the road to Damascus." A small minority will be chosen along with the good angels for eternal salvation. They will constitute the City of God, and will live forever in heaven in perfect peace and happiness. But that city is not of this world. No earthly city or state can be said to be representative of or even part of the City of God, not even the Commonwealth of the Hebrews or the universal Catholic church, although each may prefigure and announce the City of God.

Niebuhr and others have found certain references in Augustine that suggest an association of the visible church with the City of God. Niebuhr acknowledges, however, that Augustine recognizes that the visible church is not coterminous with the Eternal City. Nonetheless, some Protestant theologians have continued to challenge the view of others that the visible church is the only perfect society on earth. For his part, Augustine offers scant basis for concluding that earthly society can be transformed into the City of

God or that mankind alone can "separate the wheat from the tares before the time of the harvest."[1]

Augustine's conclusion is that the majority of mankind, essentially all those who are not of the elect, joined by the devil and his angels, are members of the earthly city, fallen and unredeemed. Their hearts are fixed only on material goods and earthly enjoyments. They are at home on this earth, not pilgrims on a long journey. States and kingdoms of this world are part of the earthly city, spread throughout the world. The earthly city is dominated by self-love and the heavenly city by the love of God. The two cities are not to be equated with state and church. Instead, Augustine uses the two concepts of self-love and love of God, first, to criticize the pagan political order and especially the Roman Empire and, second, to sketch in the broad outlines of a Christian political order. The two cities are commingled on earth, and mankind will not actually be separated into the elect and the unredeemed until the end of time.

It is misleading to suggest that Augustine wrote only of the City of God without reference to earthly societies. His thinking was too much grounded in classical thought to neglect problems of the individual and society. Man is a social being. The *ecclesia* is a society of believers, and the world outside it is a community of sinners. Society is natural to man and the legal order is remedial. The purpose of government is to maintain internal order, protect against external threats, and preserve tranquillity. God created one single man, Adam, so that men might learn their need for and dependence on society. They pursue self-fulfillment in society. On this Augustine is in accord with classical thought. In society men seek recognition and applause, but true virtue requires humility, not self-pride. Here Christian thought prevails over the classical view. Augustine counseled the nuns at Hippo that true pride looks to the pursuit of good works. True righteousness based on the love of God is different from virtue, which requires the praise of men.

The source of virtue for Augustine, in contrast with its source in Plato and Aristotle, is the "perfect love of God" expressed in love of one's neighbors. Love, not justice, is the defining term.

1. Quoted in Herbert A. Deane, *The Political and Social Ideas of St. Augustine* (New York, 1963), 36.

The four aspects of virtue are temperance, fortitude, justice, and prudence, all defined in terms of love. Love must be preserved "entire and incorrupt" (this is temperance); maintained through all conflict (which is fortitude); its precepts recognized not only for individuals but for groups in society (justice—political parties cannot love each other, but they can pursue justice); and guarded against craft or fraud (prudence). The full attainment of virtue is possible only in the life to come. For the Christian, true justice consists not only in equity and fair dealing but also in benevolence. We are enjoined to love all men even though we are not able to do good to all men. A clear sign of the inner misery of a flawed and wicked man is his anxious quest for power and dominion outside himself. The basis for morality is the Golden Rule stated in negative form: Do not unto others what you would not have others do unto you. Justice is an approximation of love; it substitutes for love in the political order.

Augustine's discussion of justice combines classical and Christian views as he suggests that men in the earthly city are guided by the shadow or image of justice in the human heart. Men are not required to obey an unjust human law as judged by the standards of natural law and divine law and ultimately the eternal law. Among states, love of honor and glory have the appearance of virtue. The Romans at least suppressed other goals through love of country. Through love of country they came to rule the whole civilized world, thus receiving their reward. They were honored in literature and history throughout the known world. Yet crimes such as the murder of Remus by Romulus at the founding of Rome were also committed in the name of glory and the naked desire for power. Despite evidence of treachery and deceit even within the family, the City of God offers some measure of hope and happiness even if postponed for life beyond history.

The Confessions, Augustine's autobiography, is on the surface an account of his conversion to Christianity and along with it his continuing spiritual struggles and ordeals. Some also interpret the book as an account of mankind's pilgrimage from evil to good and from unbelief to belief. Others see it as humanity's attempt historically to discover a way of understanding reality from the standpoint of the divine. Augustine appears to be saying that the individual can by calling on memory become conscious of his own existence in history and of himself as a subject of history.

In Augustine's achievement of self-awareness, some historians see a turning point in the intellectual and spiritual history of Western man.

Augustine wrote during a period of the duality of church and state. The persecution of the Christian church by the Roman state continued into the fourth century from Nero to Diocletian. This persecution led Christians to see the state as negative and repressive. Nonetheless, they held to their traditional political and religious creed: "Render unto Caesar the things that are Caesar's and unto God the things that are God's." Because true justice is found only in the heavenly city, the citizenry must obey the laws of the earthly city provided they are not required to abandon their faith. It would be fair to say that the Christians half rejected and half accepted the state; this attitude set them apart from the Greeks and the Romans.

In 312, seven years after the Diocletian persecutions (303–305), the Emperor Constantine converted to Christianity. By the time he died in 337, Christianity was one of two official religions, and in 380, it was proclaimed *the* official religion. Augustine never discarded the classical view of the state, namely, that it is the highest social community. However, for Augustine the state is also a coercive order sustained by force and ruling on the basis of fear of pain and punishment. It seeks not to make men good or virtuous but to restrain citizens from evil. At best it provides not the good life but political order. The noblest expression of the state is not of this world but is the City of God. Only when the elect are raised to the City of God can man realize the virtues proclaimed by Plato and Aristotle. Such a transhistorical perspective permitted Augustine to look steadily and critically at actual states, to consider what they can and cannot do and how far they can go.

Finally, Augustine dealt more directly with war and relations among states than either Plato or Aristotle. It is impossible to find a trace of militarism or the glorification of war in Augustine comparable in any way to that of the German romantics. Nearly every one of his references to civil or international war is voiced in sorrow. On his death in 430, Augustine's own city of Hippo was under siege and was later destroyed by the Vandals. His writings reflect the fallibility of man and the state in war and peace. He described the war of the early Romans against their mother city of Alba as an act of "restless ambition." Nonetheless, Augustine doubted the time would ever come when wars would cease and men would beat their swords into ploughshares. Wars among nations, classes, and sects would go on until the end of history. He rejected the pacifism of many church fathers, such as Tertullian, Origen, and Lactantius. Perpetual peace is simply not attainable in the earthly city.

Wars occur in internecine quarrels within the earthly city as one side seeks to impose its will on another. Peace is only a temporary truce in which the victors satisfy their ambition, greed, and lust at the expense of their victims. A good ruler will refrain from wars of aggression, conquest, and plunder and engage only in just wars. Wars are just when they are defensive, as with the early wars of the Romans. The legitimacy or justice of war requires that the decision for war be made by the appropriate authority. An offensive war can be just if fought for reparations for wrongs committed or to recover property wrongfully taken from the state seeking redress. But even just wars are tragic events. Thus war is evil but, like the work of the jailer within a society, may sometimes be necessary. With Cicero, Augustine affirms that war is defensible when its goal is survival. Faced with a choice between the sanctity of treaty commitments and survival, states are in the presence of a terrible dilemma. By implication Augustine suggests the choice may have to be survival. Wars are inevitable given greed and lust for power and man's fallen state. War can at least serve the purpose of punishing evildoers.

Augustine recognized the contributions the Roman Empire had made through *pax Romana,* but he also warned against the self-defeating nature of imperial expansion. What does war and conquest gain for the conqueror or the conquered except "the inane pomp of human glory"? There will always be hostile nations beyond one's borders. "The very extent of the empire . . . produced wars of a more obnoxious description—social and civil wars—and with these the whole race has been agitated, either by the actual conflict or by the fear of a renewed conflict." As Augustine explained, everyone will admit that a man "of middling circumstances" who is content with his small estate, family, and neighbors is happier than the rich man with anxious fears and insatiable covetousness. He asks, "Is it not better to have a moderate stature, and health with it, than to attain the huge dimensions of a giant . . . and when you attain it find no rest, but to be pained the more."[2]

Augustine's ideal world order is a world made up of small states, each satisfied with its moderate territory and limited power so that all might live in harmony and peace. The controlling principle of such a society would be the balance of power. International society would be made up of states with moderate ambitions and roughly equal in power. In war as in peace they would respect the interests of the conquered as well as the conquerors, thus maintaining a basic equilibrium. If there had to be a world empire, it would be better for the Romans and those they conquered to join together by consent rather than by conquest.

> Had this been done without Mars and Bellona, so that there should have been no place for victory, no one conquering where no one had fought, would not the condition of the Romans and of the other nations been one and the same, especially if that had been done at once, which afterwards was done most humanely . . . namely, the admission of all to the rights of Roman citizens . . . and if that had been made the privilege of all which was formerly the privilege of the few, with this one condition, that the humbler class, who had no lands of their own, should live at the public expense.[3]

The late Herbert Deane acknowledged that the course of Roman history might have been different. Conflict and civil war had destroyed the Roman Republic and with it civic freedom through the rise of dictators such as Pompey, Marias, and Caesar and the autocratic rule of emperors such as Augustus. Deane wrote of the lust for rule as the vice most characteristic of the Romans. "The lust for rule . . . was found more concentrated among all the Romans . . . subdued under the yoke of slavery, the others worn out and wearied."[4] With the passage of time the *libido dominandi,* which had been characteristic of only a few rulers, became the hallmark of all. Augustine admitted that Augustus, who had taken away the liberty of the people, infused new life and esprit into the

2. *Ibid.,* 169, 171.
3. *Ibid.,* 171.
4. *Ibid.,* 170.

aging republic, initiating what Augustine described as a "fresh regime."

In such a world, what can mankind hope for and seek? After enumerating all the failings of human justice, Augustine sets forth certain positive normative ideas for the state and politics that would be reiterated by Niebuhr and other thinkers in the twentieth century. He writes about proximate justice and degrees of justice and injustice in human society. Modern critics might say Augustine had given in to relativism by such a view. It is clear that the precepts and practice of proximate justice are deficient when judged by the standards of the City of God, but they may be superior to no justice at all. In politics, justice is sometimes a matter of lesser evils. Rome's justice based on honor and glory falls short of the ideal but nonetheless mitigates the harsh features of the ruthless pursuit of power. The most earthly states can do is to realize a semblance of virtue growing out of men desiring to be well thought of while being fearful of punishment and desiring praise. Because we are surrounded by evil and have evil within us, the highest achievement of man is to achieve some semblance of the teachings of natural law. They retain at least "impressions" of God's truth. Vestiges of true justice remain imprinted on the mind of fallen man. Human ideas of justice are imbedded in political institutions. A sense of prudence can direct men's decisions in the path of justice. Even prudence cannot withstand the two most stubborn human defects: ignorance and misguided will. But prudence can point the way to realistic approximations of justice that men may prove capable of achieving.

We may ask, finally, in what way Augustine is relevant to our age. As we have seen, he was the first political realist. Since the mid-1950s, the story of international studies has been nothing so much as a debate between realism and its critics. Augustine's principal focus was on man, created good but corruptible. For Augustine, man's corruption takes the form of self-pride and self-centeredness wherein men, fearing domination by others, seek domination over their fellow men. According to twentieth-century thought, the process of domination and counterdomination is called the security-power dilemma.

Augustine's concept of the state and justice reflects his political realism. Whereas Aristotle saw the state as the arena within which the individual achieves virtue, for Augustine the state restrains the citizen from evil. The state is an instrument of coercion. Only in the City of God can the individual attain the good that Plato and Aristotle praised. War is unceasing in the City of Man, interrupted only by temporary truces. Having drawn this conclusion, Augustine goes on in sorrow to describe war as a tragic event. His ideal international order is a system of small states preserved by the balance of power. Insofar as morality among states is concerned, Augustine writes of proximate, not absolute, justice. Justice is an approximation of love, and love is too pure for the painful compromises of politics. All these insights from Augustine bring us closer to the reality of contemporary politics. They demonstrate how classics can remain relevant in the present.

Six

Thomas Aquinas (1225–1274)

Thomas Aquinas is "the official philosopher" of the Roman Catholic church, especially as identified with the Jesuits. Pope Leo XIII described him as "the Catholic thinker." His most systematic and significant work is *Summa Theologica,* published in 1270 and organized in eight volumes. This work provided the intellectual foundations for much of subsequent Catholic thought. About ten years earlier Aquinas wrote *Summa Contra Gentiles: Of the Relation of Human Reason to the First Truth of Faith,* which speaks of a twofold source of truth, one attained by rational inquiry and the other transcending all reason. He also wrote *Commentaries on the Politics of Aristotle* and some seventy other minor works. Most commentators consider Aquinas the greatest theologian of the Middle Ages.

Aquinas was born in 1225 in Aquino near Naples, Italy. His family hoped he would follow an ecclesiastical career and perhaps become bishop of Naples. Instead, he pursued his early education in the famed Benedictine monastery of Monte Cassino and at the University of Naples. In 1243 he was admitted to the Dominican Order of Preachers against the wishes of his family. Their opposition was so great that they proceeded to kidnap and hold him for almost a year, during which he studied and transcribed Aristotle on logic. Later he went to Cologne to study with Albertus Magnus. The two continued working together, teaching and writing in Paris. Aquinas died at the age of forty-nine, his life caught short but his writings an enduring legacy of Christian thought.

Aquinas made clear his indebtedness to Aristotle, in particular to Aristotle's emphasis on political participation. He recognized the *polis* as the community in which man could realize his highest purpose, or *telos*. He saw the end and purpose of the *polis* as virtue and viewed politics as a noble enterprise, not, as in Augustine, a means of remedying and mitigating original sin. Whereas Augustine saw life as a struggle, Aquinas defended the role of reason with cool detachment and untroubled serenity. However, the world in which he lived was hardly serene. With the adoption of Christianity as the Roman Empire's official religion, church and state became indistinguishable, especially in the East, culminating in the Byzantine and Russian empires and the Eastern Orthodox church. With civilization centered in the Church, some accepted the visible church as coterminous with the City of God, in marked contrast with Augustine. The conviction spread that if all men were Christians peace would reign. In 800 Pope Leo III proclaimed Charlemagne Holy Roman Emperor and endorsed a crusade to establish a *pax Christiana*. The goal was a Christian empire, and by the twelfth century the church under Pope Innocent III ruled. Societies became thorough-going theocracies.

The involvement of the church in statecraft raised a perennial moral and political problem. At issue was defining the respective spheres of spiritual and secular authority. In the eyes of some papalist writers the absence of a universal theocratic government was explained by maintaining that spiritual authority would have been weakened by the exercise of temporal power. Critics of the papacy could oppose ecclesiastical interference in political affairs without denying the existence of a sphere of higher rules above the temporal domain. In Walter Schiffer's words:

> The "international state" of the Middle Ages was based on two contradictory principles. The unity of this state was established by the existence of the common Church, which was supposed to exercise an authority higher in kind than that of the temporal rulers. Impartial justice and Christian love, which were supposed to be the guiding principles of the spiritual sphere, seemed to require the absence of power and politics in the exercise of the spiritual authority. The latter's exalted character appeared to be the better preserved the higher it rose above the sphere where those considerations were of importance and the more it limited itself to applying its means

> of coercion only in the interest of man's salvation. But if the spiritual authority were to exercise any influence in the lower sphere of temporal rule, if the attempt to maintain peace and order in the Christian world were to have any effect, then the Church necessarily had to participate in the political struggle and to use its means of compulsion in a manner which produced results in the political sphere. The spiritual authority thus became inevitably entangled in secular affairs. This entanglement tended to eliminate the distinction between the higher and the lower, the spiritual and the temporal spheres, and particularly to deprive the spiritual power of its character of impartial guardian of justice. The secularization of the Church and its identification with temporal power became the particular objects of attack for the political and the theological movements leading to the breakup of the system of medieval unity.[1]

Another authority wrote:

> The most outstanding characteristic of the international organization of the Middle Ages is *the Pope's right of coercion toward aggressors or disturbers of the established order.* It is an unusually serious problem, for two ideological principles are here in open conflict: the notion of the *ratio divina,* the moral sense of the teachings of the Gospels, and the juridical necessity immanent in every positive order to have its decisions respected. Natural law here comes into opposition with the precepts of positive law and a theoretical antagonism leads finally to a supreme crisis of the hierocratic system.[2]

It was possible to argue that even when the popes applied natural law to a concrete case, they were establishing a positivist legal order. In so doing they inevitably introduced an element of arbitrariness. They depended on force for the maintenance of the legal system. Thus a contradiction in the medieval system became apparent between a higher sphere of spiritual law and the actual exercise of power by the popes. Their constant interference in the political order clashed with their claim to represent a higher spiritual order. Schiffer concludes by arguing that

1. Walter Schiffer, *The Legal Community of Mankind* (New York, 1954), 25.

2. Michael Zimmermann, "La Crise de l'organisation internationale à la fin du moyen âge," *Academie de Droit International, Recueil des cours,* XLIV (1933), 355.

> authority was exercised in the interest of worldly, political goals. Generally these authors [the critics] criticize not the idea of unity of the Western world but the means by which the Popes attempted to maintain this unity. Examples of this interpretation of the historical development leading to the disappearance of the medieval system can be chosen at random. For instance, an international lawyer writing at the end of the nineteenth century speaks of the grasping worldly ambition of the Popes and declares that while the Emperor failed for lack of power to constitute himself the universal pacificator and arbitrator, the Pope failed in the same task for lack of impartiality. It was the same idea expressed in other words when it was said that "the Pope by aspiring to universal dominion, fell to the position of a sovereign among sovereigns" and "became a disturbing influence in the political system of Europe."
>
> Toynbee . . . traces the downfall of the medieval papacy back to the fact that the latter became [in Toynbee's phrase] "possessed by the demon of physical violence which it was attempting to exorcise," and that it substituted the material for the spiritual sword.[3]

The papacy lost much of its standing as the exemplar of a universal spiritual force once it intervened in the affairs of state. The public opinion of Western Christendom turned against it, and unity was eventually shattered. In this time, distinctions between the secular and sacred orders became more difficult to make. The church functioned as any other secular state, subject to the same constraints and compulsions for peace and order as other political societies. Its mission was no longer confined to faith and morals. It became the dominant force in the world of the balance of power. It confronted challenges not only within the Catholic world but from Islam sweeping across the Near East, Middle East, North Africa, and Spain. Islam was the carrier of new ideas and a translator of older traditions, including Aristotle. Papal supremacy was also challenged by movements such as the Albigensian and Waldensian heresies. Society was moving from agrarianism to commerce, from country to town and rural communes to cities. The Middle Ages, often considered the Dark Ages, was actually a time of dramatic change, and it was this world in which Aquinas taught and wrote.

3. Schiffer, *The Legal Community of Mankind*, 25.

The twin purposes of *Summa Theologica* are the systematic survey of Christian theology and the elaboration of philosophical and social judgments based largely on Aristotle. The inquiry directs attention to three fundamental areas of concern. Part One is devoted primarily to reflections on God and the creation of the world and of man. Part Two presents Aquinas' views on the nature of man. Part Three deals with Christ and the sacraments. The second section has greatest relevance for the philosophy of international relations as it takes up such questions as, What is the proper end of man? What laws and principles guide him to this end? What virtues or vices give impetus to or impede his realizing this end? On these and other questions, Aquinas reviews some of the earlier commentary and offers his own conclusions.

In his discussion of politics and the political community, Aquinas follows the thinking of Aristotle. He departs from the pessimism of Augustine, as had other medieval writers. With Aristotle, he finds that man's goal in the state is the good life and that the common good is above the good of the individual. In opposition to Augustine, he argues that the political community is a natural institution based on reason that would have existed whether or not man had sinned. Some Christian critics have questioned certain Thomistic precepts, such as, "The perfect community is the state" and "The individual is to the perfect community as the imperfect is to the perfect." In questioning such views, which have their source in Aristotle, we must remember that *state* in Aquinas' time did not mean what it meant to Aristotle or to modern philosophers. It was a much vaguer concept, less weighted in the direction of totalitarianism. It was not the intention of either Aristotle or Aquinas to impute perfection to the institutional state. In their times, ethics, politics, and society were not separated but were part of an integrated whole. Indeed, politics was but a branch of ethics.

Still, Aquinas' focus was less concentrated on the individual and individuality and more on the good of the community. The aspect of politics that concerned him most was law. For Augustine, the law above all laws is the eternal law, which is beyond the reach of man. Divine law is the expression of the eternal law and is accessible to men. Natural law contains the precepts essential for the attainment of virtue and the good life. Human law is positive law, or what we describe as legislation for the ordering of society.

Men are not bound to obey an unjust human law if it is contrary to divine and natural law. Thus the possibility of revolution is acknowledged.

Like Augustine, Aquinas locates eternal law, known only to God, above all other law. Natural law is next in the hierarchy of operative laws and makes possible the participation of man as a rational being in the eternal law of God. Men seek to apply natural law in accordance with prudence. Divine law is a spiritual version of law accessible to both Jews and Gentiles. Most of Aquinas' discussion of politics occurs in those sections of *Summa Theologica* concerned with the relation between divine and human law and natural and positive law. More broadly, Aquinas defines law as "an ordinance of reason, for the common good, promulgated by one who has the care of the community."

The main themes in Aquinas are reason and faith and reason and nature. Aquinas' great achievement is in synthesizing Aristotle's conception of man and nature with Christian thought. His most famous expression illustrating this synthesis is that grace does not annul nature but perfects it. Scholasticism draws together reason from philosophy and revelation from theology. In his interpretation of Aristotle, Aquinas took a middle position between the Latin Averroists, who subordinated faith to reason, and the Augustinians, who subordinated reason to faith. The natural order is good because it was created by God. Man was created in the image of God and despite the Fall retains a residual capacity for virtue and reason. All things in nature aim at some good. The end that man pursues is assigned him by nature.

Law and politics depend on experience and tradition. That moral problems are complex does not preclude knowing right from wrong. Prudence for Aquinas is not the balancing of evil alternatives in a tragic choice, as it is for Augustine and later for Niebuhr, but rather is the highest expression of man's humanity. It consists in "reason perfected in the cognition of truth." It is "necessary for the prudent man to know both the universal principle of reason and the singulars with which ethical action is concerned." Prudence freely answers "to the specifications which the situation requires."[4]

4. Josef Pieper, *Prudence,* trans. Richard and Clara Winston (New York, 1959), 20, 25.

For Augustine the best international system was one of small and medium states with moderate ambitions. Aquinas agrees with most aspects of Augustine's plan for a decentralized international system, but he goes further and makes yet more exalted claims for a world order. The Stoics had introduced the idea of a brotherhood of men. Aquinas found in natural law "the common order of reason," which enables man to transcend his own political order. As man according to Aristotle is completed in the *polis,* states are completed in the international community. The perfection of states politically in the international community has its parallel spiritually in the visible church as the guardian of natural law. By the time of Aquinas, Augustine's City of God comes to be equated with the Roman Catholic church. Aquinas seems almost euphoric about the visible church applauding "the marvelous disposition of Divine Providence," which made use even of the Roman Empire to spread the Christian gospel.

In pointing to the corruption of the papacy, Luther and Calvin were quick to identify the waning of the Christian empire. Protestants in France, Holland, England, and Germany revived Augustine's concept of a more decentralized international system.

The debate over reason and natural law continues down to the present. Nature is no longer defined from the standpoint of teleology. Discoveries in physics and astronomy call Aristotelian natural science into question. Niebuhr places Aquinas in the category of "idealist" in contrast with Augustine the "realist." For Niebuhr natural law more often than not "conceives a system of norms without considering that historical norms are influenced by the contingent power factors in an historical situation."[5] Defenders of Aquinas maintain he was more aware of contingent factors and the need for political prudence than Niebuhr suggests. They note that Dante, not Aquinas, suggests world government as a practical political possibility. Aquinas asserts that if world unity is to occur, it will come on the basis of various expressions of functional community.

A year before he died, Aquinas set aside his work on the *Summa,* saying, "All that I have written seems to me nothing but

5. Reinhold Niebuhr, *Man's Nature and His Communities* (New York, 1965), 49.

straw . . . compared to what I have seen and what has been revealed to me."[6]

The relevance of Aquinas for the contemporary world can be traced in his defense of reason. Like John Courtney Murray, Aquinas argued for the role of a residual form of reason that survives in our time. He placed community above the individual, perhaps reflecting his allegiance to Aristotle. Aquinas would have been as impatient as Murray with what the latter called "moral ambiguism," identified with Niebuhr. As for church and state, one central issue is the problem the church confronts when it assumes the functions of the state. If it becomes just another "sovereign among sovereigns," it faces all the temptations of the secular order: self-righteous policies, grasping world ambitions, and confusion of natural and positive law. Aquinas seems closer than Augustine to identifying the visible church with the City of God. Perhaps Aquinas' major contribution is in his definition of prudence, in which he again departs from Augustine and the later realists. Prudence for him is not the balancing of evils but the highest expression of man's humanity and his quest for the common good. Yet Aquinas also acknowledges that prudence must be responsive to the specifics, or what he calls the "singulars," of each situation. On other issues his reasoning is less satisfactory, as when he places community above the individual and when he views the community as a natural institution based on reason.

6. Quoted in Josef Pieper, *The Silence of St. Thomas: Three Essays,* trans. John Murray and Daniel O'Connor (Chicago, 1965), 40.

Seven

Niccolò Machiavelli (1469–1527)

Machiavelli is a name that evokes wide-ranging commentaries and interpretations. For Leo Strauss the writings of Machiavelli are the point at which political philosophy broke with the classical tradition, and especially with Aristotle, and took on an entirely new character. Harvey Mansfield, Jr., describes Chapter 15 of *The Prince* as "a fundamentalist assault on all morality and political science, both Christian and classical, as understood in Machiavelli's time." Herbert Butterfield finds that "no other treatises on the art of politics have so stirred . . . controversy in every generation. . . . To some he has appeared the malevolent counsellor of tyrants; to others the noble spokesman of a nation's liberties. To some he has seemed the most hard-hearted of realist politicians, while others have called him rather a philosopher who was more modern than the times would bear."[1] Whether we see Machiavelli as a "teacher of evil" or the founder of realpolitik or a prophet and defender of nationalism or republicanism depends on which of a long list of commentators we have read and accepted.

Son of a physician and born into a middle-class family, the young Machiavelli pursued humanistic studies. In 1498, at age twenty-nine, he entered the service of the Florentine Republic as

1. Leo Strauss and Joseph Cropsey, *History of Political Philosophy* (2nd ed.; Chicago, 1972); Introduction to Niccolò Machiavelli, *The Prince,* trans. Harvey C. Mansfield, Jr. (Chicago, 1985), x; Herbert Butterfield, *The Statecraft of Machiavelli* (New York, 1962), 10.

secretary of the Council of Ten and secretary of the Second Chancery. He was ambassador of Florence to France, Spain, and Germany, and his dispatches and reports foreshadowed the diplomacy of the future. At the time he wrote, Italy was divided into five smaller states: the kingdom of Naples in the south, the aristocratic republic of Venice in the northeast, the duchy of Milan in the northwest, and Florence and the papal states in the center. The Medici coup d'état in 1512 and the restoration of the ruling house brought about the downfall of the Florentine Republic. The popes of the time, while scoundrels and profligates, consolidated the papal states into a permanent force in central Italy.

In 1513 Machiavelli was imprisoned and tortured for conspiracy. Cardinal Julian de Medici brought about his release, and in return Machiavelli wrote *The Prince* for private circulation. He dedicated it to his patron, a member of the Medici family. Prudence dictated that its general publication be delayed until after his death; it was more widely published in 1532. After his release Machiavelli had fled to Saint Andrea and a small family estate, where he wrote *Discourses on the First Ten Books of Livy*. Throughout, his sources were more the nonphilosophical classical writers: Livy, Tacitus, Plutarch, Polybius, and Xenophon. He followed leaders such as the Holy Roman Emperor Frederick II and Philip IV of France, who emphasized those official acts of the state that were considered necessary but amoral. In 1525, after thirteen years in exile, he was recalled to government service by the Medici, but two years later they were overthrown.

In 1525 Machiavalli wrote the *Florentine History,* dedicated to the Medici pope Clement VII, and later a report for Clement on the fortifications of Florence. He also wrote plays, including *Mandragola,* which has been described as a farce, "brilliant but obscene," and the equal of Molière. In his foremost inquiry he sought to answer the question of how power is acquired and how it is maintained.

Machiavelli is said to have been a witty conversationalist and storyteller, a good father and an unfaithful husband, a literary artist but not a systematic thinker. His works are scattered and diffuse, but their principles and axioms are remarkably coherent. He wrote at a time when cruelty and murder in government were commonplace. Good faith and truthfulness were considered childish scruples. Force and craftiness were the keys to success. Machiavelli's contempt was reserved for men like Pietro Soderini, who was too virtuous to employ the ruthless methods that could have thwarted the Medici coup. His admiration, by contrast, was for Cesare Borgia, who was without scruples. Looking back, Machiavelli attempted to explain the successes of leaders. He used a kind of political calculus, taking examples in which a certain political proposition brought success and other propositions produced negative results.

The main focus of Machiavelli's work for moderns is the search for order and unity within politics, not in some external or transcendent principle as in Plato or Augustine. He offers a set of do's and don'ts for political success. He provides shrewd insights into political situations, cool judgments of the resources and temperament of political rivals, tough-minded estimates of the limitations of policy, and prescience in forecasting political events. As for methodology, his approach anticipates the inductive method of Francis Bacon.

However, it would be wrong to suggest that Machiavelli wrote only about politics. He was concerned with such subjects in political philosophy as the nature of man, the definition of values, the state, glory and virtue, and conflict. For Machiavelli, man's nature is essentially evil and unchanging. He writes of man descriptively, not normatively, as Plato and Augustine had done. Consider his observations. Man is a being of insatiable desires and limitless ambitions. Man's primary desire is self-preservation. He seeks immediate rewards. He follows authority figures. He is inflexible. At the same time, man is capable of social cooperation, but clever leaders can manipulate him. Because of his evil nature, cynical rulers are able to mold and shape him. Man's nature is many-sided. Although he is selfish and indolent, he is also industrious and self-denying. He is open to all the normal processes of socialization; he can be educated.

Insofar as human values in politics are concerned, Machiavelli appears to part company with Plato and Aristotle. The supreme end of politics is the security and well-being of the community rather than the higher moral ends portrayed in the classics. The social and political consequences of political acts are more important than the moral intent of the decision maker. For Machiavelli both the intent and the consequences are likely to constitute good and evil inputs and outcomes or some subtle mixture of the two.

Machiavelli was for the most part indifferent to moral philosophy. He preferred the life of action with its moral dilemmas and moral paradoxes. Ends and means intertwine in subtle ways. For example, the individual's personal morality depends on the security afforded him by the immorality of the state. Wars of defense by the state assure the preservation of freedom for the individual. Machiavelli never doubted or questioned certain actions by individuals that were grounded in personal morality. Conventional morality for the individual could be justified as necessary and possible, especially for the common good.

Machiavelli was born and died a Christian. His attacks on the Church were intended to be anticlerical rather than antireligious. His hostility was directed at the Church for standing in the path of unity for Italy. He also criticized the scandalous lives of the popes. Indeed, he sometimes favored classical paganism over the religion of the Church. The highest end and value for man was glory, which Machiavelli defined as acts remembered and cherished by men. The brief yet glorious life of an individual or a commonwealth was better than the long history of mediocre men and societies. The greatest glory for man is realized in such acts of imagination as founding a religion, establishing a commonwealth, commanding armies, and creating literature of enduring value.

Glory depends on man's *virtu,* and here we come to the essence of Machiavelli's normative thinking. What is *virtu?* For Machiavelli it is the quality of the soldier in battle. It is manliness, self-discipline, purposefulness, determination, bravery, boldness. In war, victory depends on the struggle between *virtu* and *fortuna,* identified as chance, capriciousness, or change. In peace, the rational control over the course a society takes also depends on the victory of *virtu* over *fortuna,* suggesting that intangibles or imponderables such as the character of a nation or national morale shape its destiny. One may ask what produces *virtu* and glory in a commonwealth. Machiavelli answers that the education of a people and the innate qualities (*telos*) of its leader are decisive. Especially in the *Discourses,* he argues that a republican society such as the Roman Republic, where liberty flourishes and is defended by a citizens' army, is conducive to *virtu.* Thus the good society for Machiavelli is linked with *virtu.* The threat to the good society is an excess of commercialism. In such a society the conditions of glory are almost certainly lacking.

Further, conflict was a vital concept for Machiavelli. It is a universal and permanent condition in society stemming from man's nature. The traditional classical and medieval view had discounted the recurrence of conflict and made a strong appeal for harmony. Harmony, faith, and reason were the trinity of medieval thought. Early thinkers had sought social institutions that would eradicate conflict. Aristotle had said that matter at rest is more natural than matter in motion. The perennial form of conflict was conflict between the common people and the great and the powerful. Notwithstanding, Machiavelli refused to define the perennial struggle among social and political groups in economic or class terms. Rather, the true cause of domestic and international struggles is the lust for power and domination. The aristocracy seeks to dominate and the masses to overturn the power holders.

Nonetheless, Machiavelli, following Polybius, also argued that conflict and power can be used for socially useful ends. Power can be channeled and limited in a regime such as the Roman Republic by law and authority. Rivalry between the patricians and the plebeians can be played out constructively in the Senate or other popular assemblies. This is the message of Machiavelli's *Discourses.* By contrast, Florence was a corrupt state. It was an atomized society in which each man looked out only for himself. In such a political order, religious sentiment and civic honesty decline. Avarice takes their place.

In Machiavelli's world, the state is the most important instrument for containing and channeling man's selfish nature toward socially desirable goals. Through the state, man gains security. Machiavelli uses medical language in describing the state, but he really sees it as a mechanism. The state has no higher end or spiritual purpose than its preservation. Policies of reason of state (raison d'état) are the prudent and calculated actions of statesmen for security ends and secular aims. They are not supranational goals. However, Machiavelli seldom if ever used the term *reason of state.*

The Prince and the *Discourses* present two types of state based on the number who rule: monarchies and republics. Machiavelli identifies three types of monarchy: limited as in France, despotic as in Turkey, and tyrannical as in Syracuse. Republics are mass republics (Athens), balanced or democratic republics (Rome), or aristocratic republics (Venice). Between monarchies and republics, he identifies two unstable forms of government, oligarchies and plebiscitary monarchies. Machiavelli classifies states further by the way power is acquired—through expansion (Rome), preservation of power (Sparta), corruption (Florence), or *virtu* (the Roman Republic).

Machiavelli then asks what is required for good government. Good government depends on a strong military for security, economic prosperity, the recognition of merit, public service for those who seek glory, and regulation of luxury. Citizens must know what they can and cannot do and the legal consequences of their actions. There must be a rational system of law. Civic virtue and perhaps even civic religion must be cultivated.

Machiavelli sometimes wrote about politics in the language of war. Politics, much as war, requires preparedness and flexibility, decisiveness, surprise and deception. Most political situations are conspiratorial and counterconspiratorial. Sometimes leadership in politics resembles that of the conduct of diplomacy, calling for foresight, secrecy, and initiative. Machiavelli was the great realist, but he kept one foot in the classical world. Montesquieu read the *Discourses.* Through Harrington and Sydney and the seventeenth-century English republicans, Machiavelli bequeathed the idea of representative government to the founding fathers. Burke, Tocqueville, Hobbes, and Spinoza all recognized Machiavelli's genius. He was also the father of military thinking, influencing thinkers from Maurice of Nassau to Karl von Clausewitz. He combined pessimism about human nature and cynicism about human behavior with a vision and hope for the good society incarnate in the Roman Republic. Most important, he was the supreme spokesman for the political craft.

For the contemporary era, the test of Machiavelli's relevance is whether the world as it is supports his analysis. Given ethnic conflict and ethnic cleansing, the breakup of the Soviet empire, and the problems and dilemmas facing American policy makers, the answer would seem to be in the affirmative. States continue to place the safeguarding of their security above unqualified internationalism. As for policy makers, they are urged to consider the political consequences of their acts rather than good intentions alone. In the world as it is as against the world as it might be, choices more often than not involve moral dilemmas and paradoxes. For it remains true that the possibilities of personal morality sometimes depend on the immoral actions of the state, as in certain military actions.

In short, the issues Machiavelli raised are still at the center of international politics: morality and power, republicanism, and war and diplomacy. Machiavelli's importance may depend less on whether he represents a turning point in political theory and more on whether his observations fit the problems with which today's policy makers and citizens must contend.

Eight

The Seventeenth Century

Grotius (1583–1645)

The seventeenth century was an era of international relations giants whose influence continues down to the present day. Grotius (Hugo de Groot) is called the father of international law. Hobbes's writings display undisguised candor regarding power and the state. John Locke can be considered the exemplar of liberalism in international relations. Their viewpoints cover the spectrum of political thought to the present.

Grotius was born in Delft, Holland, where a statue in the center of the town square commemorates his life and works. The Dutch had gained independence from Habsburg Spain and established the Dutch Republic. Grotius, a child prodigy, received his early education from his father, a Dutch patrician known for his civic pride. At the age of eleven, the son was admitted to the Faculty of Arts of the new Protestant University of Leiden. At sixteen, he was admitted to the bar at The Hague. At twenty-four, he was named deputy attorney general of the highest law court in Holland. In 1624, he was appointed pensionary of Rotterdam, thus entitled to represent it in the Assembly. He gained recognition as a poet and dramatist and as a historian and jurist. He was the true Renaissance man. About this time he wrote *The Freedom of the Seas,* part of a larger work published later. In it he sought to show that no authority can claim sovereignty over the high seas, thereby angering both the Spanish leaders and James I of England.

Grotius' life story is a chronicle of triumphs and tragedies. Serious problems began for him when he bet on the wrong horse in a political dispute over whether the Dutch provinces should be a loose federal union or consolidated under the House of Orange. Grotius' ally, John van Oldenbarnevele, a grand pensionary, lost and was executed in the struggle with the stadholder, Prince Maurice of Orange. As a result, Grotius was sentenced to life imprisonment. His wife smuggled him out of prison in a box disguised as a shipment of books. He escaped to France, where he received a pension from Louis XIII. He lived by his writing and then returned to the Netherlands, from which he fled again after a year. Queen Christiana of Sweden appointed him Swedish ambassador to Paris, and he spent his next ten years as a diplomat.

The story of Grotius' life is also one of paradox. While he wrote in a time of religious decline and sought to substitute the classical tradition for theology, he crusaded for the restoration of Christian unity. Although no one would question his many-sided intellectual qualities, interpreters differ on whether he was a creative thinker, innovator, and unquestioned father of international law or a rather conservative synthesizer of the work of others. He was an optimist and a rationalist in a time of profound pessimism, the early seventeenth century. His theological outlook led to conflict with Protestants and misunderstandings with Catholics and Deists. He sought peace while at the same time propounding a doctrine of just war, describing war as a lawsuit carried on by armed forces. He pointed to ways of obtaining justice through war, including defending property, regaining possessions, and punishing criminal offenders.

Whatever the differences of opinion over his contributions, Grotius continues to be called the father of international law. Both Martin Wight and Hedley Bull identify him as the founder of one of three major perspectives in international relations (Machiavelli and Kant represent the two competing views). Grotius was a contemporary of Hobbes (1588–1679), who represents "the challenge of power to right."

In describing the Grotian view of international relations, Wight and Bull make a distinction between solidarity and pluralism. Grotius wrote of the solidarity or potential solidarity of states constituting international society with respect to the enforcement of law. According to pluralism, states lack the kind of solidarity Grotius attributes to the state system. They agree only on certain minimum purposes that fall short of the achievement of consensus on the enforcement of international law. In a word, Grotius was a solidarist, others were pluralists. One example of the difference between the two viewpoints appears in attitudes on just war. Grotius wrote about *jus ad bellum,* arguing it is possible to distinguish the just from the unjust cause of war. A twentieth-century international lawyer and pluralist, Lassa Oppenheim, whose international law treatise as revised by Hersh Lauterpacht became the standard text in the field, challenged this view by showing that war has long been the prerogative of sovereign states. Oppenheim maintained that Grotius' thought fell more in the realm of ethics than international law.

The Grotian view of just war is also offered as an alternative to two other views, namely, the pacifist view that no war can be legitimate and just, and the militarist view that any war is legitimate. What these two views have in common is a denial of international society as such. In broad terms, the activating cause for just war for Grotius is injury received. Three more specific legitimizing causes are self-defense, the recovery of property, and punishment of the offender in such acts. From World War II to the present, these solidarist concepts have been written into positive treaty law and enshrined in the Pact of Paris of 1928, which outlawed war, the Covenant of the League of Nations, and the Charter of the United Nations. The Grotian view excludes one kind of war from *jus ad bellum* and sanctifies another. According to the solidarist view, just war is war "to enforce fixed rights." In a word, it is war to maintain the status quo. Wars fought for unjust causes are wars to add land and territory, to punish refusal of marriage, to impose a regime on others against their will, and preventive war. (Contemporary observers might ask if this would apply to imposing Communist or democratic rule on a divided people.) Grotius sought to stem the tide of a people's lack of restraint in going to war and prosecuting it with more cruelty and brutality than barbarous forces and invaders. It is also true that the laws of war were generally permissive in the seventeenth century. To counter these trends Grotius undertook to give war by international society a unique character.

Pluralists such as Oppenheim sought to impose restraints on the conduct of war in *jus in bello.* Whereas pluralists have had serious doubts that either states or international society can distinguish a just from an unjust war, they believe it is possible to state what constitutes lawful conduct *in war.* War for jurists and pluralists such as Oppenheim is a political act. My state's offensive acts are defensive when seen from my national security needs. For almost thirty years a committee of the United Nations sought to arrive at an acceptable definition of aggression and finally abandoned the task.

A corollary to Oppenheim's view is that international law is indifferent to the purposes of war. Once war breaks out, however, the parties must be made subject to the rules of war and to principles of just conduct. Ironically, here Grotius and the pluralists move in opposite directions, for Grotius maintains that states fighting in the name of international law are not subject to the same inhibitions and restraints as the offenders. For Grotius, belligerents acting in a just war may kill and injure the enemy and rob and rape his citizenry. Indeed, war for a just cause even overrides the obligations a party assumes in an alliance and treaty. Such acts may illustrate Oppenheim's argument that where the preconditions of the Grotian order do not exist, its influence in practice can be detrimental to a just international order. Substitute for the Grotian view President Bush's new world order and arguments about the law of war continue down to the present. Pluralists, especially in the eighteenth and nineteenth centuries, assumed a position of neutrality with respect to just and unjust parties in war. They sought to contain the struggle without judging the parties. The one exception was intervention for humanitarian purposes, as with the European powers seeking to protect Christians in Turkey in the Crimean War or Westerners in China during the Boxer Rebellion. But such actions were not based on law.

Opposed to the pluralists, Grotius found the basis of international law in natural law. For him, judgment proceeded from the fact that natural law is the source of certain fundamental concepts that underpin international law. Law is seen as universal, and justice is determined by right reason. Natural and international law fill the void left by the decline of ecclesiastical law. Because it is universal, natural law binds all human beings, individuals as well as states. It affects the rights of the citizen to bear or not bear arms. Whether states agree or not, natural law, and therefore international law, determines whether war is just or unjust, humanitarian intervention is justified, and war and violence are crimes or police actions.

Pluralists, by contrast, find the basis of international law in the consent of states and in custom and treaties. Law must be validated by the consent of states. International law for the pluralists is by and large restricted to the Christian and European states. It is unrealistic to think that all the world's states, with their manifold customs and commitments, will comply. Only states have rights and duties in international law because only they can give their consent. States still have the right to go to war, and international law comes into play in determining justice in the conduct of war.

Grotius' most successful and popular book, *The Truth of the Christian Religion,* was published in 110 editions for seamen impressed in foreign countries. It was translated into all the European languages, Irish, Hungarian, and Arabic. Despite Grotius' religious commitment, he sought to escape from theology in his writings on international law. Religious controversies were receding into the background. Grotius sought to return scholarly endeavors to the works of antiquity. A spirit of admiration for the classics spread through Europe. Interest was revived in Plato, Aristotle, and the Stoics. A return to naturalism and rationalism such as had failed in the fourteenth century was occurring. Mathematics and the physical sciences received renewed emphasis. Jesuit writers such as Francisco Suárez acknowledged the human origins of government while continuing to defend the historic role of the papacy.

Religious and secular writers alike, with certain exceptions, cut the ties of natural law with theology. Johannes Althusius went back to Aristotle in depicting man as a social animal. He and others argued that the association of men in groups was a natural phenomenon. In this, their ideas were more Aristotelian than scholastic, even when they invoked the tradition of Aquinas. For them society was seen as an intrinsic part of man's human nature. They rejected the idea of society as an "artificial animal," as Hobbes conceived it. Underlying every association was a social contract, which took the form of a tacit agreement. A *consociato* was equated with Aristotle's community.

In society, people came to be "dwellers together." They were bound together by a twofold law: 1) between the members of society; and 2) between them and society's authority, limiting and controlling its power. Through such concepts, Althusius and the

French Calvinists planted the seeds of representative government and democracy. They asked what the basis of consent in a federal structure is, and they found the answer in natural law. However, Calvinists did not detach natural law from religion as Grotius did.

The social contract, then, was seen as a compact between groups, not individuals. Althusius discussed five kinds of authorities: the family, the voluntary corporation, the local community, the province, and the state. In more advanced societies, these underlying associations are the contracting groups. Each group takes upon itself the regulation only of such acts as are necessary to its purposes, leaving all the rest to the so-called lower or more primitive groups. Thus social groups or authorities come into being through a series of social contracts. All social and political relations are reduced to consent or compact, foreshadowing the idea of the consent of the governed.

The state is but one of these groups, and it comes into being by the association of provinces or local communities. It is different from all other groups because of its *majestas,* or sovereign power. Sovereignty resides in the people as a corporate body. They cannot pass it on to a ruling class. However, the state bestows power to various administrative offices. Between the two groups—the state and the administrative offices—another and different contract is exchanged, requiring efficient governance. Failing to succeed in establishing efficient governance, the administrative officers forfeit their power, which then reverts to the people. Althusius' formulation was the clearest statement of popular sovereignty to date. It set forth a postulate that conflicted with the ideas of Jean Bodin, who believed sovereignty resided in the monarch.

Looking back as he set out to write *The Law of War and Peace,* which was published in 1625, Grotius observed a world dominated by religious wars. The conduct in war was cruel and barbaric. Grotius employed the Prolegomena to elucidate the philosophic principles of his work. They constitute the search for a fundamental or natural law on which the civil law of a nation rested. The fundamental or natural law was binding on every nation because of its intrinsic justice. There had been such a law in Christian political thought, but Christian unity was breaking up and the authority of the Church had declined. Neither the authority of the Church nor the authority of the Scriptures could provide an effective law binding alike on Protestants and Catholics.

With his humanistic training Grotius went back to an even earlier, pre-Christian tradition of classical natural law. Critics of Stoic philosophers such as Carneades had maintained that all human conduct is governed by self-interest, foreshadowing Machiavelli as well as the pluralists in international law. As a result, law is a mere social convention based on utility and prudence. To this Grotius answered that because men are inherently sociable (Kant was later to write of man's "asocial sociability"), the maintenance of society is a major utility that cannot be measured alone by the private benefit of individuals. Therefore, the maintenance of the social order is an intrinsic good, and conditions required for that purpose are as binding as private ends. Certain broad principles of justice are natural, that is, universal and unchangeable. Upon these primary principles societies establish domestic or municipal law dependent on good faith in the sanctity of covenants. International law depends on the sanctity of covenants among rulers.

The law of nature is a dictate of right reason. There is nothing arbitrary in natural law any more than in principles of arithmetic. The dictates of right reason are whatever human nature and the nature of things require. Natural law in this sense provides a rational and scientific method for arriving at valid propositions for positive law. Thus in Grotius one finds a mixture of idealistic optimism and realism based on history. His task may have been made easier because concepts such as sovereignty meant little to the Dutch Republic. He was at least in part a product of the era of rational systems of law and politics in the seventeenth century. Science reigned, and thinkers such as Grotius and his contemporaries Hobbes and Spinoza derived axioms, theorems, and corollaries, which were applied to human relations. Ethics was cast in the form of a geometrical demonstration. Forgotten was the difference between necessity in geometry and necessity in law. Necessity in law, in contrast to geometry, is subject to all the vagaries of *fortuna* (accident or chance). Grotius was more aware of such limitations than others—so much so that another international lawyer, Samuel Pufendorf, criticized him for not seeing that math and morality have the same characteristics of predictability and certainty. Grotius' response was that no one can demonstrate that political and legal axioms hold good eternally. The law of nature is primarily an idea or a model. Human existence may approximate the model, but the two are not equatable. The idea of the scientific method was to reach its height in Descartes' *Discourse on Method,* which left its mark on the social sciences for centuries.

If we ask what the relevance of Grotius is to our times, the question should be reformulated. It should become the question of the relevance of international law as such. The answer will satisfy neither the sciolist nor the cynic. All the euphoric views about the transforming character of international law were shattered in World War II. Yet in dozens of areas international law remains operative and effective: trade, extradition, citizenship, the law of the sea, travel documentation, and countless other subjects. Nevertheless, the controversy recurs between those who claim too much and those who acknowledge too little about the relevance of international law.

What can be said is that from Grotius to Charles de Visscher scores of first-rate minds have devoted themselves to international law. The exchange between the solidarists and the pluralists is but one example of the classic debate between idealists and realists. It is a false argument to insist that international law has the same characteristics as domestic or national law, but it is also wrong to believe that the major principles of international law are universally accepted.

That such a discussion has engaged minds of the quality of Grotius and Oppenheim is a sign that the issues are fundamental. Questions are continuously being raised. Should the United Nations and the United States continue their mission in Somalia? Are those who fight for the United Nations in effect fighting a just war and therefore immune from the constraints that limit those who by committing aggression are fighting an unjust war? What happens when two enemies apparently believe they are engaged in "a holy war"? These and other questions go back to the writings of Grotius and demonstrate his relevance even today.

Thomas Hobbes (1588–1679)

Thomas Hobbes was a lawyer by profession. He studied the writings of Aristotle at Oxford University and mechanical science in Paris. He described human nature as made up of passions, forces, and motives. He focused on what was dynamic in human behavior. At Oxford he was brought into contact with the Occamites, the followers of William of Occam, author of the simplifying concept of Occam's razor. He turned their nominalism into the idea of the sanctity of the civil state, introducing the concept of civil order by social contract. Men in a state of nature exchanged a life that was "poor, nasty, brutish, and short" for a political order made possible by the Leviathan. After leaving Oxford, he became a tutor to William Cavendish, later second earl of Devonshire, and gained the opportunity for sustained scholarship. His first literary work was a translation of Thucydides, and later he completed the translation into Latin of three of Francis Bacon's essays. In 1640 he left England for France on the eve of civil war and associated himself with a group of scientists and philosophers called the New Mechanists, led by the friar Marin Mersenne. Later he was tutor to the Prince of Wales, who was to become Charles II, and who was then part of the English royal court in exile. After eleven years in Paris he returned to England, where in 1651 he published *Leviathan*. He also wrote a history of the English civil war, a defense of his religious views, and a translation of Homer.

The full title of *Leviathan* is *Leviathan; Or, The Matter, Forme, and Power of a Commonwealth Ecclesiasticall and Civil*. The Commonwealth, he wrote, was an "artificial animal" created by an act of compact or social contract. Hobbes introduced the secular theory of moral and political obligation as a substitute for the divine right theory. The sovereign or government once established by voluntary contract gained the right of command over all things temporal and spiritual. Hobbes argued that such centralized control was historically necessary for self-preservation and order in society. The division of authority between church and state—the doctrine of the two swords—had produced only unending strife in a Kingdom of Darkness. The opposition of church and state was the cause of the bloody civil wars that had disrupted England and the Continent.

Hobbes described the state of nature as a realm in which man is governed solely by natural passions. Conflict in the state of nature is inevitable. Each individual clashes with all others as do other kinds of natural bodies in "free motion." For these reasons life in the state of nature is indeed "poor, nasty, brutish and short." Also fundamental is the struggle for power. Hobbes speaks of a "general inclination of all mankind [for], a perpetual and restless desire for power after power that ceases only in death. And the cause of this is not always that a man hopes for a more intensive delight . . . or that he cannot be content with a moderate power: but because he *cannot assume the power and means* to live well, which he hath present, without the acquisition of more" (*Leviathan,* Chap. XI).[1]

In the Commonwealth, man surrenders nature's liberty in return for the liberties government may allow him. "Man may be willing," Hobbes writes in Chapter XIV, "when others are so too, as far forth, as for peace and defense of himself as he thinks it necessary to lay down his right to all things; and be contented with so much liberty against other men, as he would allow other men against himself." It follows that "to lay down a man's right to any thing, is to divest himself of the liberty, of hindering another of the benefit of his own right to the same."

Hobbes concludes that the Leviathan fundamentally partakes of two qualities. First, the Leviathan is a mortal god. It is the embodiment of reason and morality. Where there is no Commonwealth there is no justice or injustice. It is a hidden and often obscured truth that the state is the source of law and morality for the citizenry. Second, where there is no coercive power, there is no Commonwealth. Men have grief in coming together if there is no power to overawe them. "Even if a majority of men were seeking only security," they would use force and seek power, suspecting others of hostile designs. Twentieth-century thinkers were to call this the security/power dilemma. In the absence of government, man is in "a condition of mere nature," and this is descriptive of the relations among states and kings.

Hobbes's contention that the relations among states and kings are in "a condition of mere nature" presages the clash between realists and idealists. Realists would certainly accept Hobbes's explanation that international politics in particular gives evidence of a general and persisting inclination for states to seek power. They would not find amiss the reference to "a perpetual and restless desire for power after power that ceases only in death." For individuals the empirical evidence is readily at hand. Have we not observed once powerful but now retired captains of industry in the

1. Thomas Hobbes, *Leviathan,* in *The English Works of Thomas Hobbes of Malmesbury,* ed. Sir William Molesworth (11 vols.; London, 1839–45), III, 147.

twilight of life struggling to maintain and extend their influence? In everything they do, from seeking victory in bocce ball to gaining full recognition for their philanthropic gifts, they compete for recognition and power. They demonstrate an increasing quest for power "that ceases only in death."

Further, Hobbes maintains that power is bound up with security. Men and nations seek power and organize the instruments of force because they are fearful that others may dominate them. Here different interpreters find explanatory value in different theoretical propositions. Some argue that all men possess the impulse for acquiring power. They possess an *animus dominandi,* a natural, animal-like instinct to gain power as an end in itself. Others, as we have seen, link security and power. Because we are insecure, we seek power to safeguard ourselves, our territory, or our possessions. Hobbes would seem to group himself with those who believe in the security/power dilemma, although he writes of "all mankind" as inclining toward a "restless desire for power after power." Idealists deny that the inclination toward power is a persistent reality. Rather, they describe it as an archaism carried over from an ancient past. In the post-Enlightenment era, reason and science are transforming human nature and thereby the possibility of war and strife. Moreover, communication and cultural relations are drawing men ever closer.

On two points, Hobbes appears to place himself squarely in the midst of profound intellectual controversy. The first is his view that the state is the source of morality and justice. At first glance, most moderns reject this idea as being the embodiment of totalitarianism. Too recently we have witnessed Stalin and Hitler making claims for communism and national socialism that at least on the surface are reminiscent of Hobbes. For Stalinism and nazism the state tended to be the source of morality. The eradication of five million kulaks and six million Jews was carried out in the name of the Soviet and National Socialist states. The state provided moral justification for what otherwise would have been seen as grossly immoral. Could one not say that the Leviathan as mortal god established what was right and wrong? Much as Plato's critics found that the idea of the philosopher king was antidemocratic and totalitarian, some of Hobbes's critics make that charge. Forgotten by Hobbes's critics was the individual's voluntary relinquishment of certain rights through a compact or social contract.

Moreover, the individual gives up these rights seeing that others are willing to do the same. The individual gives up as much liberty as he is willing to give up for others. These several political equations distinguish the Leviathan from Stalin's or Hitler's state.

The second controversy that Hobbes enters concerns the relation of coercion and the state. It is the state that coerces the individual to do what he would otherwise resist doing. The power and the mystique of the mortal god inspire civic response. Men must stand in awe of the state. Lacking the sense of awe, they will continue to behave toward one another as they did in the state of nature. They cooperate and accept the rights of others because of the potential for coercion by the state. By confronting these issues, Hobbes plainly has a message for society in the 1990s.

John Locke (1632–1704)

The final act in the drama of English politics in the seventeenth century occurred with the Glorious Revolution of 1688, the so-called bloodless revolution. James II had promoted Catholicism, but the majority of Englishmen were Protestant. Events confirmed that they rejected republicanism and a commonwealth (which had led to Cromwell's military dictatorship) and chose instead a monarchy controlled by Parliament. In this way the succession of William and Mary was confirmed. It ushered in class government, which in the eighteenth century produced social and cultural benefits but also some of the worst abuses such a government had known. Still, the political system was called representative, and compared with any other European government, it had to be called liberal. The succession settlement closed a chapter in the relationship of religion and politics. Never again would the two be united in England. The Toleration Act proved to be the only basis for permanent peace between the churches.

Thus the intellectual temper in the time of John Locke (and Halifax) was different from what it had been fifty years earlier. Even though Hobbes was not religious, he devoted half of *Leviathan* to the problem of *imperium* and *sacerdotum*. By contrast, Locke was in a sense a child of the eighteenth century born ahead of his time.

Even though his personal life was shaped by Puritanism, he was indifferent to theological dispute. Halifax was a thoroughgoing skeptic, but Locke was too much of a philosopher for that. He made compromises with logic as he defended individual rights. Locke's two treatises on government were published in 1690. Their purpose was to defend the Revolution of 1688. Locke's thought had its roots in Thomas Hooker's *Ecclesiastical Polity,* which was a summary of English political thought at the close of the Reformation. Hooker's political theory in turn was inspired by Aquinas.

The medieval tradition as it had been developed by Hooker was the basis for the constitutional ideals of the Revolution of 1688. In *Leviathan* Hobbes had found political absolutism to be a necessity to assure peace and order. Locke's *Of Civil Government* was meant to refute Hobbes. Locke asserted that king and parliament were responsible to the people or the community governed. Power in such a political order had to be limited by the moral law and constitutional tradition as well as the history of the realm. For Locke community determines government, but for Hobbes a preexisting community was a fiction. Hence for Hobbes ideas like representation and responsibility required the force and sanction of a sovereign power.

Locke attacked Hobbes's state of nature. Locke saw the state of nature as one of "peace, good will, mutual assistance, and preservation." The only defect of Locke's state of nature is its lack of organization, courts and magistrates, and written law. Right and wrong in Locke's state of nature are determined eternally. Positive law merely provides an apparatus for the enforcement of existing rights. Locke asserts that man's right to his own property and his duty to respect another's property *exist.* They are not dependent for their creation on the dictates of the Leviathan. However, rights such as life and liberty are not provable but are merely self-evident axioms. In opposing Hobbes's concept of morality instituted and enforced by the Commonwealth, Locke asserts that morality gives law, not law morality. Why, then, is morality binding? Here Locke draws an analogy with property and natural law. Society exists to protect private property, but property is a right society does not create. By nature property results when man mixes his labor with land. In this Locke is as egoistic as Hobbes. Individual self-interests for both are compelling. As for methodology, Locke joined a psychology that was empirical with a theory of science that was rationalist.

Locke's importance for modern times rests less on his learning or logic and more on the uses that have been made of his precepts and ideas. To speak of self-evident rights to life, liberty, and estate or property is neither good history nor good logic, but it was to be profoundly influential in the formulation of the Declaration of Independence. Not for the first time, flawed ideas and axioms had an enormous impact on history, in this case the history of the United States.

From the standpoint of international relations theory, Hobbes's and Locke's opposing pictures of the state of nature have been important. Almost every professor in an international relations course makes some reference to the Hobbesian and Lockean perspectives. Given his penchant for careful empirical observation, Hobbes could hardly have been persuaded that the state of nature was anything other than "poor, nasty, brutish, and short." The Lockean world view was of a state of nature characterized by "peace, good will, mutual assistance, and preservation." It has turned out that the Hobbesian and Lockean concepts of nature and human nature are ready made for contemporary thinkers. The realists embrace most of Hobbes's theory. Idealists find in Locke confirmation of their beliefs about man and international society.

To carry the comparison further, Locke finds that the one defect in the state of nature is the absence of organization, courts and lawyers, written law, and penalties and rewards for those who act. It is striking that Lockean idealists in contemporary international relations theory follow a similar path. They call for international peace through international law and organization. If Hobbes had been convinced that international organization was needed in the 1990s, he almost certainly would have written about coercion and enforcement. Perhaps out of the interplay of these two perspectives, we may gain deeper insights into contemporary international problems.

It is important to observe that twentieth-century debates over the nature of international politics hark back to Hobbes and Locke. Those that maintain that international relations are marked by the struggle for power base their thinking in part on Hobbes. Man's nature reflects the qualities that Hobbes identified in his state of nature. By contrast, those who look forward to a world of "peace, good will, and mutual assistance" rest their case on Locke. Even today, theorists of international relations debate whether Hobbesian or Lockean viewpoints offer the more valid picture of reality. This fact is one of the premises on which the return to the fathers that characterizes this book is based. Two seventeenth-century thinkers are important not only for the substance of their political theories but also because of their continuing relevance in the late twentieth century.

NINE
The Eighteenth Century

Eighteenth-century thinkers have exercised a direct influence on contemporary international relations. Among those whose impact is most enduring are Adam Smith, David Hume, Jean-Jacques Rousseau, Montesquieu, and Edmund Burke. The century coincided with the Age of the Enlightenment, although political thinkers such as Hume and Burke were exceptions to the prevailing optimism of the age. Most Enlightenment writers looked forward to a world where a new international order of reason and science would usher in peace and progress.

Adam Smith (1723–1790)

Adam Smith was born in Kircaldy, Fifeshire, near Edinburgh. He was the son of the controller of customs. He received an M.A. degree at the University of Glasgow and was appointed a fellow at Oxford University. He was a student of Francis Hutchinson, the father of the philosophy of moral sentiments. In 1776, he advised Charles Townshend on the plan to tax the American colonies. Like many other eighteenth-century thinkers, Smith traveled to France, where he met and drew on the thinking of physiocrats and philosophers. Throughout the eighteenth century, Paris nurtured some of the most important thinkers of the Enlightenment. The Scottish thinker went on to Geneva, where he entered into conversations with Voltaire. Returning to Scotland, he became a professor of moral philosophy and professor of logic. His first writings were a series of articles on rhetoric.

His first major work was *The Theory of Moral Sentiments* (1759), which deals with the interrelationships of men living together in communities. It describes the role of sentiments in moral judgment. Smith defines *sentiments* as passions, affections, and feelings that find their place in consciousness somewhere between strict reason and sophisticated political calculations. Smith contended that man was endowed with human sympathy and empathy for others, even on matters involving his own interests. Man's desire for sympathy from others leads him to practice a measure of beneficence in human relations. A society's survival depends on there being a minimum of understanding and justice for its people, which enhances the possibility of cooperation and shared feelings.

The Theory of Moral Sentiments is primarily about men living in communities. Because of empathy and concern, we are all both participants and spectators, externally in our sentiments for others, internally in ongoing judgments of ourselves. Sympathy leads to a more socially conscious community. Religiously, it is embodied in an optimistic Deism. We see ourselves mirrored in the responses we receive from others. To some degree at least, we recognize our real selves in the attitudes that others display toward us.

Justice for Adam Smith is commutative justice. It is negative rather than positive justice. It is refraining from doing injury to another person or doing harm that might be avoided. The state is the best instrument for the enforcement of justice. To Smith, fear and justice are linked. States in international relations are inspired to cooperate because of fear, especially in international relations of the growth of military power in another state. With such an insight, Smith appears to take a Hobbesian approach to international politics. The more patriotism the individual feels for his state, the more disdain he has for other states. In the absence of a world sovereign, all nations live in fear and dread of one another. Any significant increase in the power of other nations leads to conflict or war. States accord only that measure of justice to others that they expect others to show for them.

Smith deliberates over the two divergent viewpoints that were advanced in the famous debates over Rome's policy toward Carthage. In one debate after another, Cato rose in the Senate and declared: "It is my opinion that Carthage ought to be destroyed." Scipio Nascia opposed Cato and urged that Carthage not be destroyed. Smith comes down on the side of Scipio Nascia, both from the standpoint of justice and from that of the consequences of history. He reminds his readers of Rome's decline following the brutal and total destruction of Carthage, including the killing of all its men, women, and children. At the same time, he is no utopian or universalist. Love of country, Smith writes, is not derived from the love of all mankind. Rather, love of one's country is patriotism for its own sake. He adds that men fear their immediate neighbors more than more distant ones. This view suggests that Smith had a geostrategic perspective on international relations.

Smith's *Inquiry into the Nature and Causes of the Wealth of Nations* is unquestionably his greatest work. Written in 1776, *The Wealth of Nations* is important for at least three reasons. First, it collects a vast array of economic data on Greece, Rome, Great Britain, and France. Second, *The Wealth of Nations* is the most comprehensive analysis of Smith's time—and according to economic historians such as the late Jacob Viner of all time—on the relationship of the individual to the economic process. Third, it is one of the most powerful criticisms ever of governmental intervention or interference in the economy.

It would be wrong, however, to believe that Smith saw no role at all for government. In fact, he pointed to significant areas in which it was essential that government play a positive role. In a word, Smith was not an all-out proponent of laissez faire, even though he is frequently portrayed as the high priest of nonintervention by the state in the economy. Government has a role in the enforcement of justice. It is responsible for the setting of standards of weights and measures, for the stamping of commodities to protect consumers, and for the issuance of building codes. It has responsibility for the levying of taxes, for national defense, and for certain large-scale activities such as supporting a standing army and licensing the East India Company. All this suggests the idea of a mixed economy. It must be remembered that Smith approached economics as an aspect of political economy. Economics and politics, which were to be separated in the twentieth century, were part of a whole in the eighteenth century. Economics also involved household management. Smith considered his books to be objective studies of the economy, not political tracts in defense of a given form of economics. His major criticism of governmental intervention in the economy was the tendency of bureaucrats to play narrow politics with the economy or "to truck and barter," as he put it.

Economic development, as Smith saw it, depended on the interplay between a community's economic resources and the striving of individuals. Development is propelled primarily by the drive of individuals for economic betterment. This motive power or driving force is present in the individual from birth and never leaves him; it is an essential part of man's nature.

Smith also introduced into his writing the concept of the division of labor in economics. In the language of present-day economists, he talked about Fordism, the assembly line approach to mass production. He believed that the repetition of simple tasks promotes skill and dexterity. It eliminates the loss of working time in changing from one task to another. It facilitates inventions, the growth of aggregate wealth and income, and the development of labor skills. Critics ask, "Doesn't the division of labor also lead to the degradation of the individual?" "Isn't monotony in performing a single task destructive of individual initiative?" Smith believed he had found measures for counteracting such dangers. He sought to vary the dehumanizing routine of performing only one or two simple tasks a day by extending the benefits of elementary education to the workers.

Smith's view of human nature was based on a few simple propositions. First, man has an innate tendency to seek to improve. Second, he betters himself through competition. Third, the wisdom of nature is more productive for human progress and economic development than governmental dictates or public actions. Smith was against monopolies of any kind and was in favor of free competition. However, he was far more eclectic and flexible than many of his latter-day followers. In his time, he rejected the rigid models that Turgot and Hume crafted. He recognized the importance of utilitarianism as an incentive. He left room for the play of ambition and power.

Few would question that Smith was the great prophet of economic liberalism. He defended man's natural right to private property and favored individual enterprise. He saw the individual being guided as if by a hidden hand. In pursuing selfish interests, man served the common good. Significantly, with all his emphasis on the individual, Smith understood the importance of collectivities. Quite simply, he believed that the interests of the group were best served through providing first the interests of the individual. National wealth depended, however, not only on the economic power of a nation but on free trade. Every nation would benefit from free trade. Based on his conclusions about free trade, Smith stipulated that comparative nations ought not produce at home that which can be produced more economically abroad. He was an early proponent of the law of comparative advantage. He may not have recognized some of the difficulties of free trade, such as the need for economic self-sufficiency in wartime. He had little to say about autarchy and its necessity in a half anarchic international society. He may not have recognized that nations at war can ill afford to depend on others for their survival.

As for human nature, Smith had no question that man is self-centered, but he believed man is also capable of wide-ranging sympathy and some degree of impartiality. Citizens within the state often gain approbation at home by denouncing other nations. Yet breach of conduct by a nation is cause for a just war. Smith concluded that nations need not be enemies and that international harmony is possible, particularly if based on a balance of power.

It would be difficult to argue that Smith has no relevance for contemporary international relations. First, he was the foremost defender of a free enterprise economy, which has become the rallying cry for the United States and other free societies around the world. Second, he stands out as the champion of free trade. He saw economic development as closely linked with nations producing what they are able to produce best. No nation ought to produce what another can produce better and at less cost. Third, he was untiring in defending the primacy of the individual not only in the economy but in society at large. Fourth, Smith offered a view of economics that was broader than the traditional approach of economists. His approach was that of political economy, which has suffered from neglect in recent decades in the study of economics in the United States. For Smith, politics was as important as economics, especially in providing the framework for the working out of economic policies. As we have seen, he clearly acknowledged the necessary functions of government even while making a general argument against the intrusion of government into the economy. Fifth, Smith could hardly be described as a value-free social scientist. His intellectual journey began with a discussion of moral sentiments. Throughout his writings he displayed a continuing concern with moral and political ends: freedom, sympathy, and individualism. Not only did he make reference to such values but he placed them at the center of his thinking. Finally, different groups in American society at different moments have adopted Smith as their patron saint. Officials in the administration of President Gerald Ford from 1974 to 1977 displayed Adam Smith buttons on their lapels, no doubt because of Smith's free enterprise views but also perhaps because of his emphasis on values. In short, recent American history provides examples of both Smith's tangible and his intangible influence on American politics and society.

David Hume (1711–1776)

David Hume was the son of an upper-class family in Scotland. He was educated at the college of Edinburgh and first tried the study of the law. Next he undertook a business career in the office of a Bristol merchant. Neither law nor business satisfied his "passion for literature" and he went to France, where, before turning thirty, he wrote *A Treatise of Human Nature*. On returning to London he arranged for the publication of the first two volumes of the work and in 1740 the third volume. He was bitterly disappointed that the book failed to stimulate interest in the scholarly world. He concluded that only by writing in a more popular style would he gain recognition for his work. He returned to the family home in Ninewells and in 1741 and 1742 published the first two volumes of *Essays Moral and Political,* which gained for him the immediate acclaim that had escaped him with *Treatise*. In 1748, he followed *Essays* with a restatement in more popular form of the first part of the *Treatise* in *Philosophical Essays Concerning Human Understanding*. In 1751 he published *An Enquiry Concerning the Principles of Morals,* which involved a rewriting of the third part of the *Treatise,* and a few months later in 1752 *Political Discourses* appeared. In *My Own Life,* he describes *Discourses* as "the only work of mine that was successful on the first publication." With these publications, he gained recognition throughout the rest of Europe as well as in England. In 1753, he published the collected volume *Essays and Treatises on Several Subjects.*

Hume had served as secretary to General St. Clair on a military expedition to France in 1747 and on a diplomatic mission to Vienna and Turin in 1748. In 1752, he was named keeper (or librarian) of the Advocates' Library in Edinburgh. Here he was inspired to write a history of England. In 1763, the Earl of Hertford appointed him acting secretary to the embassy in Paris, where he remained for over two years. Then he returned to Edinburgh and arranged for the publication of *Dialogues Concerning Natural Religion,* which he had held back for twenty years. Hume's attitude toward religion was one of the reasons he was considered so controversial. After his death, his grave was desecrated and he was condemned for his views. In his later years he was Adam Smith's close friend and in certain respects his teacher, especially on the question of moral sentiments.

Hume sought with both his theory of knowledge and his views on politics and morals to proceed with "inferences and conclusions" drawn from "experience and history." He presented his inferences on human behavior as hypotheses that would require verification. His definition of politics was broader than present-day concepts since for him it included political economy, geography, and culture. Manners and customs are determinants at least as important as law. Government rests on opinion regarding the right to lawful power, the public interest, and property. Civilization in Europe is sustained and enhanced by the coexistence of a number of "neighboring and independent states connected together by commerce and policy." The wealth and hence the power of a people are determined by free commerce.

Hume wrote a series of essays, including "Of Money," "Of Interest," "Of the Balance of Trade," "Of Taxes," and "Of the Balance of Power." In each the gravamen of his argument is the need for the balance and limitation of power—balance in opinion, balance between interest and right, balance of labor and capitalists, and balance of commerce. He maintained that the principle of balance has been demonstrated by experience and is a precept by which all governments should be governed. In international relations, he was always conscious of the need for a balance of power for the sake of the independence of each nation and state. He referred to the idea many times, as when he wrote: "The balance of power in Europe our grandfathers, our fathers, and we have all deemed too unequal without our attention and assistance. But our children, weary of the struggle, and fettered with encumbrances, may sit down secure and see their neighbors oppressed and conquested till at last they themselves and their creditors lie both at the mercy of the conqueror."[1]

Not only is the principle of the balance of power essential for the safety and well-being of a nation or state, but it is also essential within a constitutional system and rule of law. The different branches of government must reflect the authority accorded them by an effective distribution of power. Hume cites Machiavelli: "A government . . . must often be brought back to its original principles," which means to secure a balance among the powers of government. Local government must balance national government, and the civil authority must always be superior to the military. The "higher offices of the republic" must be distributed so as not to fall into the same hands. To those who argue that small countries are better suited to limited constitutional government than large states such as France or Britain, he responds: "Though it is more difficult to form a republican government in an extensive country than in a city, there is more facility, when once it is formed, of preserving it steady and uniform without tumult and faction."[2] The debate over constitutionalism and larger and small countries continues and finds expression in American political theory in the writings of Alexander Hamilton, who favored a compact centralized regime with a strong banking and industrial base, and Thomas Jefferson, who saw the country expanding into new territory in the West.

History and experience, then, are essential to Hume's approach. History is an adjunct of moral philosophy. Through history we display certain general truths about man, politics, and society. There are causal relationships and connections of facts and values that the historian can search out. In illuminating them, Hume draws on Thucydides, Polybius, and Machiavelli. History pro-

1. *Essays Moral, Political, and Literary,* ed. T. H. Green and T. H. Grose (London, 1899), 374.

2. *Ibid.*, 157.

vides the raw material for general observations on manners, finance, commerce, arms, and arts and sciences. In his *History of England* Hume writes of "the duty of an historian to point out the proper inferences and conclusions on all these matters." He goes so far as to maintain that abstract reason without experience cannot decide or explain anything. Indeed, imagination is an important part of understanding; imagination helps us see that the future will resemble the past and that we each have a self or personal identity in an external world. Hume sought to demonstrate in his *Enquiry Concerning Human Understanding* (a revision of *Philosophical Essays Concerning Human Understanding*) that belief represents a judgment beyond the evidence of experience and is due to what he called a presumption of mind. It was this idea applied to religion and especially to the existence of God that led to much of the opposition and criticism of Hume after his death.

Hume also challenged the idea of the social contract, saying that it was a Whig idea. With the rise of the nation-state, Hume understood that the social contract was a means of offsetting the dominant view of absolute monarchy. The Whigs saw the social contract as the only basis for the rights of government. In practice, the consent of the people gave the king authority to rule. But Hume warned that it was Parliament in practice that gave or withheld such consent on behalf of the people and might thus claim excessive authority for itself. It could treat any opposition as subversive. After the publication of Locke's *Second Treatise of Government* (1690), the Whigs sought to use this doctrine to party advantage. Ironically, Hume and Rousseau, despite the title of the latter's greatest work, were in agreement here. Rousseau denounced the idea of an explicit contract, saying the sovereignty of the people is inalienable and cannot be contracted away to any person or government. However, the people can and do acknowledge the general will (*volonté générale*), which is the true social compact. It reflects the authority of the actual community and is the source of sovereignty, law, and obligation.

To summarize, Hume's methodology provides that all *beliefs* concerning facts are based on the association and relation of ideas. Men come to believe in the causal relationship between two events because of contiguity and recurrence. In a certain sense, belief equals habit. History has given man an adequate basis for formulating certain principles of human nature. However, there is wide historical variability. Hence different levels of generalization are possible. For example, gross behavior and group passion such as avarice can be identified in politics. Where the number of individuals is small, such identification or generalization is more difficult. Thus we speak in economics of "gain" or "liveliness" or the desire for "action."

Hume makes an exception to his reflections on the level of generalization when he writes about the balance of power. Thus he asserts, "It is *never* [my emphasis] right to help a power to acquire a preponderance that will render it irresistible. There must be an equal distribution of power." Based on Hume's principle, what was not right with the Soviet Union after World War II was not right for Iraq before the Gulf War. The practice of the balance of power antedates its articulation. The Greek city-states practiced it without being fully aware of the general principle. So Rome overcame Greece. Rome as an empire was not subject to it until its decline. The Italian city-states in Renaissance Italy were an ideal closed balance-of-power system in an arena of limited size. Renaissance Italy was a miniature state system. The balance was measured as if the weights in the balance were the same as on the scales of the Italian bankers. New weights and counterweights threatened to tip the scales. Venice was the balancer throwing its weight between Florence and Milan. The theorists of the balance were Machiavelli and Guicciardini, with the former more perceptive on military history and the latter on diplomacy. The way Italy could save itself from invasion was for its neighbors to be preoccupied elsewhere with one another. Machiavelli thought superficially at least about the question of what a state should do when two neighbors are at war and one neighbor threatens to emerge more powerful. His answer was to remain neutral, gain prestige, and always seek to be on the winning side.

If we were asked to state in one word or concept what makes Hume relevant to contemporary international relations, it would be his contribution to our understanding of the balance of power. With all the eighteenth century's preference for new modes of international relations, the practice remains fairly constant. Even as NATO proved a means of balancing Soviet power, President Bush's coalition in the Gulf War eventually constituted a balance of power against Saddam Hussein. Within or outside the United Nations or NATO, U.S. power coupled with that of its allies contained the Soviet Union through a balance of power.

If Adam Smith is flanked on one side by David Hume, Jean-Jacques Rousseau and Edmund Burke stand on the other side. In the eighteenth century, political theory had its center in France. Smith and Hume were representative of Scottish thinkers who sought to participate in the Enlightenment in France. Two Americans who were also children of the Enlightenment were Thomas Jefferson and Benjamin Franklin. At the outset the main focus of political thought had been on mathematics, metaphysics, and theology. Descartes was the symbol of pre-eighteenth-century French thought. Early in the eighteenth century Louis XIV characterized the French state in the words *l'état c'est moi* (I am the state). Others pointed to the specter of growing decadence. All Europe, Louis XIV said, was against him. The era witnessed a vast outpouring of books on the ancient institutions of France, European government, America and Asia, trade, and taxation. Poets like Voltaire, novelists like Rousseau, scientists like d'Alembert and Diderot, civil servants like Turgot, and sociologists and essayists such as Montaigne rose to prominence, each in his own way.

Charles-Louis de Secondat, baron de Montesquieu (1689–1755), and Jean-Jacques Rousseau (1712–1778)

Of all the French political philosophers of the eighteenth century, Montesquieu and Rousseau stand out. Montesquieu is sometimes credited with being the author of the classical formulation of the idea of checks and balances and separation of powers. He was a French provincial lawyer and nobleman. In *The Persian Letters,* (1721) he offered an oblique criticism of French manners and politics, as Voltaire was to do in *Candide.* The political theory in his most influential work, *The Spirit of the Laws,* first published in 1748, derives from Locke and the Roman law theorists. In 1734 Montesquieu wrote *Considerations on the Causes of the Greatness of the Romans and Their Decline,* anticipating Edward Gibbon's *Rise and Fall of the Roman Empire.* He praised the balance achieved between the parts of the state in the British system, wherein "the one enchains the other" and "so the whole moves together." Whereas Locke in discussing the threefold division of constitutional powers had referred to the legislative, federative (treaty making and foreign affairs), and executive powers, Montesquieu introduced the distinction between legislative, executive, and judicial powers.

Montesquieu's main objective was to explain the conditions upon which freedom depends and to contrast them with the conditions of despotism he deplored in countries like Russia and Turkey. He sought to present a sociological theory of government and law. His experiences in England and his travels throughout the rest of Europe inspired the belief that a public spirit or civic culture is a necessary condition of government. Not only a sense of civic morality but the correct organization of the state is essential, and in the eleventh book of *The Spirit of the Laws* Montesquieu sets forth his views on the separation of powers. He wrote about British institutions as a model for strengthening political liberty. He saw in England the continuation of the idea of the mixed state that went back to Plato's *Laws* and was reflected in medieval constitutionalism.

In fact, the civil wars in England had destroyed mixed government, and the nation had settled once and for all the supremacy of parliament. Thus Montesquieu's discovery of the separation of powers in the English constitution was based more on the writings of Locke, Harrington, and Bolingbroke than on his own travels and observations. Montesquieu's enduring contribution stems from his sociological relativism and his insistence that government be studied in the context of its social and political milieux. The writings of sociological interpreters of international relations such as Raymond Aron clearly reflect the influence of Montesquieu.

In this setting, Rousseau stands out as a romanticist who departed from Hobbes and Locke. He attacked absolute monarchy not by inference but in the form of a direct frontal assault. The difference between the English and French revolutions was a difference in historic political traditions. An effort was made in France to import the philosophy of Locke, but the French lacked the social and intellectual foundations on which Locke based his political theory, namely Hooker and Aquinas. The English Revolution was fundamentally a conservative revolution. Reason was harmonized with custom and tradition. In France, reason and tradition had confronted each other as polar extremes and continued in opposition to each other. Revolutionary tracts in France were written under the heel of despots and carried an undercurrent of bitterness. Reason in France was radicalized, and the tendency was reinforced by a religious factor. It must be remembered that the French clergy still controlled one-fifth of all property, and this fact fueled a strong anticlericalism. One measure of the differences between the French and English milieux was the different uses that were made of Locke's philosophy in the two countries. In France before the French Revolution, Locke's philosophy was an attack on vested interests. In England after the revolution it provided a defense of such interests.

Rousseau was a pivotal figure in all of this. A deep gulf separated him from the French Enlightenment. Diderot wrote that the "very idea of Rousseau disturbs my work as if I have a damned soul at my side." Rousseau's *Confessions* focused on the morbidities of sex and religion. He said man is good but is obsessed by a sense of sin. For this society is at fault. (Some contemporaries have revived this idea when they warn that many in the twentieth century are guilt laden.) Clearly, Rousseau was against the progress of science. He won a prize for an essay entitled "Discourse on the Sciences and Arts." Its theme is that man is naturally good but that social institutions have made him evil. Indeed, this is the core of his political theory. He wrote, "A thinking man is a depraved animal." In another connection Rousseau had praise for "the noble savage." He charged that science takes away all pieties and faith. Against the progress of science, Rousseau sought to defend such qualities as amiable sentiments, good will, and reverence. The sharing of a common life is productive of virtue. Moral virtues are purest among the common people.

Rousseau apparently saw no conflict between two of the virtues he celebrated. In *Discourse on the Origins of Inequality* he wrote of "defiant individualism." In *The Social Contract* he praised "defiant collectivism." For politics the most important idea and the highest moral value is the community. It is the main producer of virtue in the individual. Man indeed becomes human in society, an idea that seems to reflect even as it contradicts Aristotle's view of the *polis*. Rousseau was a citizen of a city-state, Geneva. He wrote: "We become men only after we have become citizens." Aristotle had argued that man achieved full virtue only within the state. Rational self-interest is not a reputable moral motive, Rousseau argued, because it excludes prudence as a virtue. (It is worth noting that while Kant agreed with Rousseau's criticism of self-interest, Adam Smith most certainly did not.) Carl J. Friedrich's book *A New Belief in the Common Man* translates some of Rousseau's ideas about the common man into a more contemporary setting.

For Rousseau, the *esprit* of the simple society is a mean between primitive innocence and civilized egoism. Whenever individuals have common interests, they form a society. Indeed, in Rousseau's intellectual schema society has the status of a moral being. Undergirding society is the general will—*volonté genérale*—that tends always to seek the preservation of the whole. The general will is the source of all law and morality. The community pursues a collective good different from the private interests of its members. It lives its own life and suffers its own fate. To repeat: the community has a will of its own, the general will. Government is merely an agent or a committee of the community. Such a view, critics say, leads to an idealization of nationalism and to sanctification of the collective will. It clears the way for Hegel and German thought. Yet it also anticipates the idea of the ordinary man in Kant. Rousseau's concept of community would be subjected to both praise and condemnation throughout the subsequent history of political thought.

The question persists as to how far one can go in claiming Rousseau has relevance for international relations. Observers find that while he seemingly agrees with Hobbes about self-preservation being man's essential motivation in the state of nature, he points as well to compassion over oppression and human suffering and especially man's pain and death. It can be argued that with this concept Rousseau lays the foundations for humanitarian actions in world affairs. On another front, he aligns himself with Locke and Hobbes in their assertion that society exists by convention and not by nature. He asks what gives legitimacy to any civil order and finds the answer in the act by which a people becomes a people through the constitution of government. There are possible contradictions between his observation in *Discourse on the Origins of Inequality* that man is isolated and alone, needing only what is required for self-preservation, and his explanation in *The Social Contract* of cooperation between men who come together to help those who are victims of floods and earthquakes. He maintains that the act of association creates a moral entity with the general will representing the interest of the community in reconciling liberty and authority. Only the particular will of the disordered person opposes the general will. Man is transformed in the civic state and begins to consult reason as the guidepost of his actions rather than desire and instinct. The general will directs the state toward the common good. The general will does not emerge full blown from the people but requires the guidance of the extraordinary man whom Rousseau calls the *legislator,* reminiscent of Plato's lawgiver. Extraconstitutional and standing apart from the government, the legislator creates the conditions and the framework for government and the original fundamental laws. Day-by-day legislation is the responsibility of the government.

Although Rousseau is less than precise, he argues that no government fits everyone's needs. A country's size, geography, culture, and resources determine its needs. Rousseau is sometimes ambivalent even about democracy. Monarchy seems inevitable in large states, democracy better for small. Aristocracy is best for moderate-size states. Republican government or an elective aristocracy with the best men chosen for specified terms of office is the best all-around regime. Such is Rousseau's paradigm of the best regime and one capable of transforming human nature. There is an uncertainty and vagueness surrounding many of Rousseau's prescriptions, but scholars in government studies at Harvard University seek to show how certain rather general precepts fit together in his philosophy, including concepts relating to the best and the ideal regime. In an era when democracy is being defined as unqualifiedly best for everyone, Rousseau's comparisons are worthy of consideration by policy makers and their spokesmen.

Edmund Burke (1729–1797)

A British thinker supplied what Rousseau's political theory lacked. For Edmund Burke the living constitution, the traditional rights and duties of Englishmen, and a rich national culture spreading out from generation to generation were the realities. They were not, as they had been for Rousseau, mere abstractions. Moreover, if readers searched sometimes for Rousseau's meaning, Burke wrote with unmistakable clarity, as when he described one aspect of social contract: "The state ought not to be considered as nothing better than a partnership agreement in a trade of pepper and coffee, calico or tobacco or some other low concern. . . . It is a partnership in all science; a partnership in every virtue, and in all satisfaction. As the ends of such a partnership cannot be obtained in many generations, it becomes a partnership, not only between those who are living, [but also] those who are dead, and those who are to be born."[3]

For Burke the historical and organic life of England was a reality and a conscious fact. It was a standard against which to measure the cruelties of the French Revolution. Burke's *Reflections on the Revolution in France* describes the brutality and violence as it unfolded. Burke separated out the general will from Jacobinism and reestablished it as a factor in conservative nationalism. For him British nationalism was an anchor, but the country was not beyond criticism; witness his strictures against Britain's policy in India and the American colonies. The general will, like Kant's categorical imperative, was a broad but unfilled category that required more specific content to approximate reality. Burke found such content in the conservative tradition while Rousseau found it in the more radical French tradition. Rousseau was critical of philosophical rationalism and natural law. His critique and denial, however, were a matter of feeling. He offered sentiment as an alternative. Rousseau lacked the intellectual steadiness of Burke and his capacity for a sustained, politically realistic analysis. It was Hume who had undertaken the task of criticizing natural law and separating the element of reason from other factors that were empirical and conditional.

Burke was not against reason or against theory as some critics have suggested. He was the most influential figure in the counter-Enlightenment. His conservatism, while sometimes overly passionate, was more progressive than American conservatism, perhaps because the United States had not experienced the feudalism that Europe had known. If reason is seen as a product of the logic chopping that lives on in some forms of analytical philosophy, Burke was no friend of reason. However, reason, as Hegel was to

3. Edmund Burke, "Reflections on the Revolution" (1790), in Burke, *Works* (3 vols.; Dublin, 1972–73), V, 203.

demonstrate, may also be equated with understanding (*verstand*) that derives from experience and tradition. Burke was the champion of practical reason, and he can be called a historical empiricist. He attacked false theories by comparing them with political practice. The touchstones of theory for him, and in particular theories about man and human behavior, were the questions, Does it suit his nature in general? Does it suit his nature as modified by his habits?[4]

Burke's view of theory and practice is remarkably similar to that of some of the contemporary international relations theorists discussed in *Masters of International Thought.* Toward the end of his illustrious career, Niebuhr liked to say he had become increasingly Burkean, particularly with regard to the Soviet Union. He came to this thinking after having passed through two earlier perspectives. In the 1930s, Niebuhr had been cautiously hopeful about communism in the Soviet Union. Later he returned from a trip to Russia disillusioned because of its tyranny and warning that the fusion of political and economic power made the Soviet regime more cruel and oppressive than the free system it was meant to supplant. Its moral and political absolutism had transformed the Soviet Union into a utopia prepared to sacrifice every human right, including the lives of five million kulaks, to its ideological purposes.

Niebuhr's evolving thought saw him moving to join those who identified international communism linked with Russian imperialism as the main threat to peace and stability in the world. Some called him a cold warrior, although he never ruled out the possibility of change. As Winston Churchill called for negotiations to end the Cold War early in the 1950s, Niebuhr entered his Burkean period. The threat of nuclear war was too terrifying, and Niebuhr, who had earlier rejected negotiations because the momentum of the communist revolutionary movement was too great, began to write about accommodation. He invoked Burke's notion of prudence or political reason as a framework for his thought. The signs of change in the Soviet Union, while not conclusive, were sufficiently tangible for Niebuhr to warrant serious attention by the

4. Edmund Burke, "Speech on the Representation of Commons in Parliament" (1782), in Burke, *Selected Writings and Speeches,* ed. Peter J. Stanlis (Gloucester, Mass., 1968), 332.

West. Communism, which Niebuhr had seen as the second great twentieth-century threat to Western civilization after Hitler, was beginning to run its course. Earlier he might have said with Burke: "It is with infinite caution that any man ought to venture upon pulling down an edifice which has answered in any tolerable degree for ages the common purposes of society."[5] As the United States floundered in Asia and the specter of a nuclear holocaust drew ever closer, Niebuhr had the courage to change in his policy for the Soviet Union. With Burke, Niebuhr recognized the need for balance in policy, and he attacked the militarization of policy including containment, just at the time the Soviet Union was changing. If he had lived, it is likely he would have attacked the massive military buildup in the Reagan administration.

Another perspective on Burke is that provided by the late Sterling Professor of Law at Yale Law School, Alexander M. Bickel. In his provocative little volume *The Morality of Consent,* Bickel made the case for the existence of two diverging traditions of political thought, one liberal and the other conservative. The liberal tradition, he wrote, was contractarian and exemplified by Locke and Rousseau. The conservative tradition Bickel associated with Burke. The liberal model rests on individual rights, the conservative on the reality of an existing society. Conservatism is "flexible, pragmatic, slow-moving, highly political."[6] It partakes of the relativism found in Justice Oliver Wendell Holmes's view of the First Amendment. It relies on the political marketplace; it expresses a mature skepticism about progress. As for the French Revolution, Burke thought of it as a "chaos of levity and ferocity." The seizure of power by the masses was no less endangering than that by kings. Foretelling the rise of Napoleon, Burke in 1790 warned the French of the soldier who would secure the obedience of the armies and become "the master of your Assembly, the master of your whole republic." When chaos prevails, the alternative of using force and violence becomes more likely.

Critics of Burke's strong response to the French Revolution often neglect his restraint in prescribing solutions to the French problem. Not only was Burke's approach pragmatic, but he proceeded with a strong sense of place and circumstance. "Circumstances,"

5. Burke, "Reflections," 74–75.
6. Alexander M. Bickel, *The Morality of Consent* (New Haven, 1975), 4.

he wrote, "(which with some gentlemen pass for nothing) give in reality to every political principle its distinguishing color and discriminating effect. The circumstances are what render every civil and political scheme beneficial or noxious to mankind." The foreign observer acts under severe constraints whenever he offers answers to the problems of another country. In Burke's penetrating commentary: "I must see with my own eyes, touch with my own hands, not only the fixed but the momentary circumstances, before I would venture to suggest any political project whatsoever. I must know the power and disposition to accept, to execute, to preserve. . . . The eastern politicians never do anything without the opinion of the astrologers. . . . Statesmen of a more judicious prescience look for the fortunate moment but they seek it . . . in the conjunctions and oppositions of men and things. These form their almanac."[7]

In summing up the case for conservatism, Bickel argued that if we "fix our eye on the middle distance where values are provisionally held, are tested, and evolve within the legal order—derived from the morality of the process, which is the morality of consent—our moral authority will carry more weight. The computing principle Burke urged upon us can lead us then to an imperfect justice, for there is no other kind."[8]

7. Quoted *ibid.*, 32, 15–16.
8. *Ibid.*, 142.

TEN

The Nineteenth Century

Three figures have tended to dominate the debate over nineteenth-century political theory. The first is Immanuel Kant, most of whose writings were published in the late eighteenth century but who is often seen as an intellectual counterweight to Georg Wilhelm Friedrich Hegel. The third figure whose influence extended across most of the nineteenth century is Karl Marx.

Two political theorists could not be more different than Kant and the last eighteenth-century thinker, Edmund Burke, discussed in Chapter Nine. The former is frequently described as the stereotypical German professor while the latter epitomizes traditional British conservative political thought. Apocryphal or not, the story is told that Kant's neighbors set their clocks when he appeared at his door at 4:00 P.M. everyday, setting out on his daily walk. Burke's writings are associated with pragmatism and political realism, and such perspectives were apparently anathema to Kant, who wrote scathingly of practical politicians: "Instead of possessing the practical science they boast of, these politicians have only practices; they flatter the power which is then ruling so as not to be remiss in their private advantage."[1] In so doing, they sacrifice and overlook the interests of the nation and oftentimes the whole world.

Lawyers and politicians make a great show of understanding the

1. Immanuel Kant, "Perpetual Peace," in Kant, *On History,* trans. Lewis White Beck *et al.*, ed. Lewis White Beck (Indianapolis, 1963), 121.

men with whom they are continually engaged without understanding the true nature of man. Kant argues that politicians and lawyers proceed on the basis of certain maxims, which are expressed in sophistries. First, seize every favorable opportunity for usurping the right of the state over its own people or over a neighboring people. Be bold; don't seek to justify actions. Violence can be glossed over more readily after the fact. Second, if your actions go sour, deny that you are at fault. If you have conquered a nation, say that the fault lies in the nature of man, who unless resisted by force will conquer you. Third, try to divide and rule. Set your followers at odds with one another. All will soon depend on your untrammeled will. According to Kant, great powers are not ashamed at revealing such principles, for they share a common immorality. Their sole approach to moral principles is their political honor—"and this honor is the aggrandizement of their power by whatever means." Kant declares: "Let us put an end to this sophism . . . and force the false representatives of power to confess that they do not plead in favor of the right but in favor of might."[2]

Immanuel Kant (1724–1804)

Immanuel Kant was born on April 22 in Königsberg (today Kaliningrad) in East Prussia. He was raised in a pietistic environment that emphasized emotionalism and the importance of the inner life in religion. He attended the University of Königsberg and became first an instructor (privatdozent) and in 1770 chair professor of logic and metaphysics. While privatdozent he published *General History of Nature and Theory of the Heavens* (1755), and eleven years after receiving his chair, he published the *Critique of Pure Reason* (1781). He compared the *Critique*'s influence on philosophy to the Copernican revolution in astronomy. His next book, *Religion Within the Limits of Reason Alone,* so distressed Frederick William II, king of Prussia, that Kant was forced to agree not to write again on religion (Kant interpreted the ruling as being for the lifetime of a particular king). He published *The Critique of Practical Reason* (1788) and other works on metaphysics. For the purpose of this

2. *Ibid.*, 122–23.

chapter his most significant work is "Eternal Peace," also titled "Perpetual Peace" (1795). In his later years he withdrew from the university, and as he declined, his students cared for him and published his writings drawn from their lecture notes. He passed away a few months before his eightieth birthday.

Kant's reputation derives primarily from his works in philosophy, where he is seen as the forerunner of Hegel. In English-speaking countries his contribution to political theory is often overlooked. Yet these writings, which grow out of his philosophical works, are an integral part of his legacy. Some have called him the philosopher of the French Revolution. He sympathized as well with the American Revolution, and from Rousseau he gained respect for the common man. Indeed, for Kant, Rousseau was the Newton of moral thinking (only Rousseau's portrait adorned his home). Accompanying his emphasis on the individual, Kant gave impetus to the secular context of law and politics and to the importance of reason and science enshrined in the Age of the Enlightenment. Especially as citizens and scholars, men were enjoined to break the shackles of authority. Whereas pre-Enlightenment thinkers had recognized the place of reason in the study of nature, the Enlightenment extended its use to man and society. Kant responded to the core ideas of the Enlightenment, but his conservatism, rejection of the right to rebellion in any general sense, and tendency toward pietism and romanticism set him apart.

Kant's general philosophy shaped his political theory. The universe for him was one great harmonious order, nonhierarchical in character despite the emphasis of thinkers such as Aquinas, who pictured it as a realm of ascending purposes. For political thinkers like Descartes, every event could be deduced mathematically from fundamental principles of mechanical action. It had been accepted that the goal of science was the discovery of mathematical relations. Descartes was convinced that theorists could discover the laws that defined these mathematical relations in much the way scientists solved a problem in geometry. How are we to explain the mind and thought of man and the relation of mind and matter or of thought and reality? These were the problems that confronted Kant as philosopher.

For Kant, human knowledge depends both on reason (for Descartes, reason was independent of sense and experience) and on sense as interpreted by empiricists such as Locke and Hume. However, despite the Enlightenment view of reason, Kant concluded that we can never know things in themselves except through moral will. For him, the universe must be seen as having two parts: the world of things as they appear to us, and the world of things as they actually are (*ding an sich*). Man can never acquire knowledge without asking the right questions. Nature does not speak to man unless man asks questions of nature. Reality is the joint product of the form prescribed by the mind and the matter inherent in the object.

The world of things as they appear through intuition and understanding constitutes the world of phenomena. The world of things as they actually are and which cannot be understood through intuition and the senses constitutes the world of noumena. The only way man can make contact with the world as it actually is is through moral will. As creatures of desire we belong to and are part of the phenomenal world. The phenomenal world is the world of cause and effect and the empirically identifiable self. However, man's moral and transcendental self transcends the phenomenal world and makes contact with the noumenal world.

The two realms are in effect the world of what is and the world of what ought to be. We can approach the former through empirical observation and the latter through an act of moral will. Man's moral obligation and will are inseparable from his freedom. Acts of moral content are possible for man because of his catching a glimpse of what ought to be (Plato's shadows on the cave?). Moral behavior is action in conformity with law. It is prescribed by reason. It is behavior dictated not by self-interest or personal advantage but by duty. It is the product of a good will.

Kant wrote of the moral imperative, which requires the individual so to act that he can will his act to be universal law. The commands of reason that impel the will are moral imperatives. Kant drew a distinction between the hypothetical imperative and the moral imperative. The hypothetical imperative directs us to something to reach a particular end identified without reference to its intrinsic value. The categorical imperative directs us in our choice of action in accordance with the intrinsic value of a goal. It directs us without regard to personal advantage, desire, or even some more ultimate goal. Again, the categorical imperative directs that man should so act that the maxim of his act could become a universal principle. Consciousness of moral obligation belongs to man by virtue of his being a moral being. Noumena cannot be explained. Science belongs to the realm of phenomena, morality to the realm of noumena. The ultimate reality is the noumenal world, which can never be known by reason or intellect alone.

When we turn our attention from Kant's philosophy to his political thought, we confront the question for which political theorists have sought an answer for two centuries. Why is it that Kant has not found a place among the foremost political thinkers in the history of Western thought? The fact is that he is sometimes excluded even from comprehensive texts in political theory. Why? Consensus on the answer to this question may be difficult to achieve given the diversity of interests and philosophies in political theory. Some say Kant was too complex and formalistic; others explain that he was best known for his commitment to metaphysics and philosophy. Those who have reviewed the various versions and translations of Kant's writings find differences in emphasis if not substance as translators struggle to determine his meaning. In early versions of "Perpetual Peace," for example, references to evil and human nature are quite explicit. A 1903 translation of Section 1, Proposition 1, dealing with secret reservations in peace treaties that contain material for future wars attributes the problem to "the evil intention . . . of using the first favourable opportunity for further hostilities."[3] The 1963 translation, by Lewis White Beck, uses the words "a tacit reservation" and "a treaty made in bad faith" but has nothing to say about man's nature.[4] A 1968 translation published in 1970 characterizes the parties to the treaty as possessing "sufficient ill will" to seize "favourable opportunities" for future wars. As for states acquiring other states through "inheritance, exchange, person and donation," the 1903 translation explains that a state cannot be inherited by another state "but that there are instances in which sovereign power can be inherited by another physical person. The state then acquires a ruler . . . not the ruler as such the state."[5] Beck's translation explains that a state cannot be inherited by another state, "but the right to govern it can."[6] On Kant's argument that standing armies must be abol-

3. Immanuel Kant, *Perpetual Peace,* trans. M. Campbell Smith (London, 1903), 108.

4. Kant, "Perpetual Peace," in *On History,* 86.

5. Kant, *Perpetual Peace,* trans. Smith, 109.

6. Kant, "Perpetual Peace," in *On History,* 87.

ished, the 1903 translation interprets him as warning that "standing armies are themselves the cause of wars of aggression."[7] The 1963 version explains that because the cost of peace becomes greater than that of a short war, the government can use standing armies to "relieve the state of this burden." But Kant also states that "a standing army is itself a cause of offensive war."[8] The 1903 version affirms that standing armies shall be abolished in the course of time; the Beck edition goes further and explains that they will be "totally abolished," while a 1991 translation speaks of their "gradually being abolished."[9] The point is not that the different translations are incompatible but that the several translators find differing shades of meaning in the text.

The core propositions in Kant raise intriguing questions about his place in the history of political thought. Where we place him depends in part on how we judge the political wisdom he displays. His first definitive article for a perpetual peace is republican government in nation-states around the world. With Hobbes he acknowledges that the natural condition of men living side by side in nature is a state of war. What can change this condition? It is not enough to end hostility. Rather, the civil constitutions of every state must be republican. Why should we expect that republican regimes would eliminate war? The reason, Kant explains, is that "if the consent of the citizens is required in order to decide that war should be declared (and in this constitution it cannot but be the case), nothing is more natural than that they would be very cautious in commencing such a poor game, decreeing for themselves all the calamities of war."[10] Kant enumerates all the miseries of war, including doing the fighting and paying the costs from a burden of debt that can never be paid off because of future wars. In a nonrepublican regime, the people not being citizens, only the head of state or the ruler decides, and he can decide on war with little personal sacrifice.

On the surface, Kant's explanation is open to challenge. He postulates the idea of the rational citizen who self-consciously evalu-

7. Kant, *Perpetual Peace,* trans. Smith, 110.

8. Kant, "Perpetual Peace," in *On History,* 87.

9. Hans Reiss, ed., *Kant: Political Writings,* trans. H. B. Nisbet (Cambridge, Eng., 1991), 94.

10. Kant, "Perpetual Peace," in *On History,* 94–95.

ates costs and benefits to himself and the nation. Yet history teaches that an inflamed public or assembly can sometimes be more belligerent and uncompromising than a monarchy or aristocratic regime. The French revolutionary leader Mirabeau offered this warning, and Alexander Hamilton was to repeat it in the early days of the American republic. Kant seeks a way out of this dilemma by contrasting democracy and republicanism. Everyone in a democracy wants to be ruler or master. Democracy is necessarily a despotism because it creates an executive power (the government) through which all the citizens may make decisions about and even against an individual without his consent. In such a system "decisions are made by all the people and yet not all the people; and this means that the general will is in contradiction with itself, and thus also with freedom."[11] Only a representative system of government makes republicanism possible, and only in a republican regime are the executive (the government) and legislative powers separated from each other. Any form of government that is not representative is an anomaly, for one and the same person cannot be both the legislator and executor of his will. Frederick II of Prussia saw himself as a servant of the state, but a democratic constitution makes this impossible because all seek to be rulers, not servants. The smaller the number of rulers and the greater their representative character, the closer a regime is to republicanism.

If one reflects on Kant's discussion of democracy and republicanism, one becomes aware how distant some of his thinking appears to be from our contemporary scene with its manifold problems. No one would question the advantages republicanism can bring in governance, but Kant seems to misunderstand democracy. Surely a democratic regime as we know it is based on the separation of powers, and indeed much continuing criticism of the American system grows out of the feeling that democracy brings deadlock because of such separation. No one can doubt that Kant has raised an important problem, but his distinctions leave questions and the content he gives to the several forms of government is sometimes more confusing than clarifying. On a related point, Niebuhr has demonstrated that Kant in writings outside the cor-

11. Reiss, ed., *Kant: Political Writings,* 101.

pus of his major philosophical writings has admitted to the corruption not only of man in nature but of rational man as well. He also notes Kant's confusion between law and morality, quoting a Kantian scholar who wrote that "if the determination of the will takes place in conformity indeed with the moral law—but not for the sake of the law, then the action possesses legality but not morality."[12] Kant's system is such that he cannot acknowledge the fragmentary quality of morality in human life with all its limits, except perhaps in his lesser writings such as *Religion Within the Limits of Reason Alone,* in which he puts forward a theory of sin. At one point he speaks of man as being "unholy enough," but then he pays tribute to a power that elevates man above himself through practical laws given by reason.

Kant's second definitive article for a perpetual peace is the basing of the rights of nations on a federation of free states. Kant extends his discussion to what some contemporary scholars define as the half anarchic international society. Nations, like individuals in a state of nature, live in fear of one another paradoxically because they are neighbors. What is the way out? For Kant the answer is unambiguously a federation of states. Why has such an international system not come about in the past? Surprisingly, Kant offers an explanation that contradicts what he seems to be saying elsewhere about reason and science. It is human depravity that is the culprit. What particular political and intellectual leaders are at fault? For one, military leaders have banished the word *right* from their vocabularies. Also, no state is bold enough to declare publicly for federation. But Kant reserves his sharpest language for international lawyers—Grotius, Samuel Pufendorf, Emmerich von Vattel, and the rest—whom he denounces as "sorry comforters" who can be quoted in defense of military aggression. As for their influence, Kant notes that there is no recorded instance of states ever being influenced by them. None of the provisional restraints on states that they discuss, whether peace treaties, military victory, or sovereign rights, can prevent a state from going to war.

What, then, is needed? Kant's answer is a federation of peaceful states that would seek to end all wars forever. More specifically, what would be the aim of such a federation? It would not be to

12. T. K. Abbott, *Kant's Theory of Ethics,* par. 7, quoted in Reinhold Niebuhr, *The Nature and Destiny of Man* (New York, 1945), 118.

gain power or coerce individual states. It would simply be to secure and preserve the freedom of each state. What would be the focus of such a federation? It would await the creation of a republic by one powerful and enlightened state that would attract other states to a federal association of states organizing themselves around the concept of international right. This concept must be joined with that of federation and must be accompanied by a prohibition of the right to go to war (the Pact of Paris, also called the Kellogg-Briand Pact of 1928, prohibited war but with little effect).

Kant's essay "Perpetual Peace" offers more thoughts concerning cosmopolitan rights, including the right to hospitality for a stranger in a foreign land. He indicts colonizers, including the early Americans, for contemptuous disregard of the rights of native inhabitants. What is the source of a modest revival of interest in Kant? At least on the surface, he appears to speak to a fractured world. Further, his philosophical system is at least partly attuned with modern analytical philosophy. He holds out hope and offers a positive message to the world's people, who recognize that many of their problems are no longer susceptible to national solutions. Yet Kant's metaphysics and much of his formal system pay no heed to the concrete international problems of our day. Broad and essentially empty analytical categories are his principal legacy. Nonetheless, our problems require that we give this eighteenth-century figure the attention he deserves but has sometimes been denied.

Kant's inquiries cover such a wide terrain that various authorities have felt called on to recapitulate what he wrote that is of fundamental importance. We might undertake such a summary by reviewing the four major propositions in ethical theory that run through his work. They are:

1. None of the presumed sources of good in the world can be defended unqualifiedly with the exception of a good moral will. Critics such as Niebuhr challenge this proposition by showing that not only man's mind and body have been corrupted but, because the self is flawed by self-centeredness and self-reference and rules all human attributes, man's will is also corrupted.

2. Man's will is good, not because the consequences that flow from it are good, not because it is capable of achieving the high purposes it seeks, but because it is good in itself or because it wills the good. But can it be shown that anyone consistently wills the

good? What is the evidence for this proposition, and how are we to assess Kant's justification of this proposition?

3. Duty is the obligation to act from reverence for law. Here Kant's ethical theory becomes confused as he substitutes law for morality. Elsewhere he speaks of the moral will and seems to recognize that law is limited by the moral consensus underlying it and that the law cannot extend beyond its moral foundations.

4. The supreme good that we define as moral can only be the idea of law itself, because it is this idea that determines the will and not the consequences. Does this mean that the idea of law is the *summum bonum* of morality? Are we done with discourse on morality, having discovered the idea of law, of which, ironically enough, Kant has been critical to this point? Suddenly Kant observes that man's capacity to experience moral obligation raises him above the animals and removes him from the realm of things as they appear to be, and he reverts to the idea of law.

In the end, Kant returns to the individual. His moral law has no more specific moral content than Woodrow Wilson's injunction to young men to go forward. Walter Lippmann asked where, how, when, and, above all, why. Kant counsels the individual to legislate for himself as if he were a sovereign making laws for the universe. From the single imperative for the individual all particular imperatives derive. Practical imperatives are deduced from moral imperatives, as with the imperative "act so as to use humanity, whether in your own person or in the person of another, always as an end, never merely as a means." Kant asserts that the conditions necessary for moral obligation include immortality, freedom, and the existence of God. Yet he never explores the interrelations of these conditions. He never asks how one's freedom can be reconciled with the freedom of others, or whether its increase leads to a diminution of someone else's freedom. He merely asserts that actions are right if they coexist with the free will of each and all according to some universal law, and that the state exists to promote freedom. His philosophy of history assumes a continuing movement from barbarism to nationhood to cosmopolitanism to lasting peace, but what about the emergence of new ethnic tribalism in our time? The cornerstones of Kant's international morality are republicanism, an enlightened citizenry, and the moral obligation for peace. One can only ask whether such a credo will prove attainable as a moral standard for the twenty-first century.

Georg Wilhelm Friedrich Hegel (1770–1831)

Hegel was born in Stuttgart, Germany, and at the urging of his parents chose to study theology at the University of Tübingen in preparation for the Lutheran ministry. However, he found Lutheran orthodoxy unacceptable and on leaving the university became a tutor. Having come to the attention of Friedrich Wilhelm Joseph von Schelling, who occupied the chair in philosophy at Tübingen, Hegel succeeded him when the latter was appointed to the chair at the University of Jena. In 1806, the Battle of Jena had devastating effects on all the universities in the region. Largely for financial reasons, Hegel left university life to become a newspaper editor and then head of a boys' school in Nuremberg. He later returned to the university world as a professor at the University of Heidelberg and two years after that was appointed to succeed Johann Fichte at the University of Berlin. He remained in Berlin until his death in 1831, in a devastating cholera epidemic.

Among the writings that established Hegel as a major figure in political thought are *The Phenomenology of Mind* (1807), *Science of Logic* (1816), *Encyclopedia of the Philosophical Sciences* (1817), and *Philosophy of Right*. He published his most important work, *The Philosophy of History,* in 1837, culminating a distinguished career.

What were some of Hegel's most important contributions to the history of thought? One was surely his delineation of the dialectical method, which is as old as Socrates. History reveals itself in a continuous and orderly unfolding. Each period in history has its own distinguishing characteristics, which unite all its aspects and institutions. The dialectical method leads to the discovery of necessity in history. The historical process proceeds by opposites, which interact along lines of a moving equilibrium. A key proposition for Hegel is that the real is the rational and the rational the real. The real is the permanent inner core of history. Philosophy helps us reconcile what lies between self-conscious mind as reason and reason as the actual world before our eyes. The erstwhile Lutheran theologian believed that God reveals himself through philosophy as the ideal system of thought. The Absolute for Hegel is both Thought and Will. Both reason and spirit pass through phases of affirmation, destruction, and reconstruction.

The heart of the dialectical method, then, is a process of affirmation (thesis), negation (antithesis), and synthesis. With the attainment of synthesis, we arrive at a new thesis or affirmation. All concepts are dialectically related. Analysis advances by a rhythm of opposition, and this, according to Hegel, is the only way the human mind can arrive at the truth about anything. Every proposition or doctrine contains elements of truth and error. Each is the product of self-centered and fallible human beings. Where others see the error of a doctrine, they formulate another doctrine that is opposite to the first but also contains elements of truth and falsity. Only a third action, or a synthesis, can reconcile the thesis and the antithesis. The same process continues as the new doctrine is seen to be flawed. Presumably the testing of each new thesis by its antithesis leads to a new synthesis that each time is closer to the Absolute about which Hegel writes. For him that Absolute is the will of God, and the dialectic is a method for distinguishing what is insignificant and transient from what is important for the long run. What exists is only a manifestation of deep-lying forces and reality.

History, in Hegel's view, is the manifestation of Reason (Hegel capitalizes *reason* throughout) realizing itself as human will. The history of the world discloses a rational process. "On the one hand, Reason is the substance of the universe." It gives being and substance to reality which otherwise would be lacking. "On the other hand, it is the infinite Energy of the universe."[13] It is present not only in the natural but also in the spiritual universe. It constitutes the history of the world. Reason immanent in history is more significant than the reason of any single individual. Freedom presupposes reason, for reason alone gives the power to gain freedom.

Hegel's successors were to substitute social class and economic forces for reason, and in the United States the dialectic method took yet another form. The idea of thesis and antithesis was built into the separation of powers in the American political system. Thinkers such as Niebuhr employed the dialectic to show how complex and conditional were the factors to be weighed in social and international relations. Finally, the dialectic was an antidote to the overly simple perspectives of international relations that often confound friends abroad. As a fledgling new state the United

13. Georg Wilhelm Friedrich Hegel, *The Philosophy of History,* trans. J. Sibree (New York, 1944), 348–49.

States was slow to undertake international responsibility, and it could afford a simple view of the world. In the 1990s, as the one remaining superpower, it can scarcely afford this attitude. In this context, the dialectic may be the area in which Hegel has made his most lasting contribution methodologically to contemporary international relations.

If the dialectical unfolding of reason in history is the ultimate reality for Hegel, the nation-state is the incarnation of the world spirit in history and the embodiment of rational freedom. The state is the actualization of the ethical idea. It is the march of God in the world. It is the presence of mind on earth. Hegel acknowledges that the earthly state is not the ideal, but he appeals for an affirmative attitude toward living institutions. Man realizes freedom by submitting to the laws and institutions of the chosen nation-state. Hegel cannot bring himself to claim primacy for the individual in moral judgments. Rather, the collective group or social morality is the embodiment of reason, and the state is the crystallization of the community. Individual consciences can never be the final court of judgment because they never or rarely agree. They can point to what may be right in a given circumstance but not to what is universally right. The individual has spiritual reality only as he participates in the state. Not individuals but universal reason creates the state. The state prescribes rights and duties. The state is absolute power on earth and is a moral organism. Whatever rights an individual has are drawn from his relationship with the state, not from his humanity or nature. World history is not the story of conquest by might but the unfolding of reason. Because the state is a manifestation of reason, every state is sovereign and autonomous in relation to its neighbors.

In day-to-day international relations, states relate to each other as particular, not universal, entities. Such relations are "on the largest scale a maelstrom of external contingency and the inner particularity of passions, private interests and selfish ends, abilities and virtues, vices, force, and wrong. All these whirl together, and in their vortex the ethical whole, the autonomy of the state is exposed to contingency."[14] Conflict among nations works itself out with particular entities determining the result. Nations are in-

14. *Hegel's "Philosophy of Right,"* trans. T. M. Knox (London, 1967), par. 331, par. 340, pp. 212, 215–16.

volved, however, in working out the dialectical unfolding of history. All actions, including world-historical actions, culminate with individuals giving substance to the act. They are living instruments in what is the expression of the world mind. They are at one with the roots of the deed even though it is concealed from them and is not consciously their aim or purpose. Thus individuals and nations become "unconscious instruments" for the world mind at work within them.

Hegel goes further in delineating what he in one place refers to as a "Moment of the Idea," namely the nation-state. In that connection, he asserts that there is only one nation that is representative of the world spirit. That nation is dominant in world history during one epoch, and it is only once that it can make its hour strike. "The history of a single world-historical nation contains . . . the development of its principle from its latent embryonic stage until it blossoms into the self-conscious freedom of ethical life and presses it upon world history; the period of its decline and fall, since it is its decline and fall the signalizes the emergence in it of a higher principle of the pure negation of its own . . . and so marks out another nation for world-historical significance."[15] In Hegel's time, it seems clear that the Prussian state was "the single world-historical nation" (although some speak of the German nation in this connection). It was God on earth, and its morality embodying the Absolute could know no restraints.

The uncompromising character of Hegel's portrayal of the state leads to the question of whether such a view leads inevitably to totalitarianism. This question has preoccupied serious thinkers down to the present, and a variety of viewpoints have been expressed. The philosopher Ernst Cassirer wrote: "No other philosophical system has done so much for the preparation of fascism and imperialism as Hegel's doctrine of the state—this 'divine idea as it exists on earth.' . . . Never before had a philosopher of the rank of Hegel spoken in this way." However, Cassirer goes on to show that in contrast with more extreme philosophies of totalitarianism, Hegel's view recognizes the constraints that art, religion, and philosophy place on the state. Therefore, Cassirer concludes: "The state remains, as Hegel says, 'on the territory of finitude.' Hegel would not subordinate art, religion and philoso-

15. *Ibid.*, par. 348, p. 218.

phy to it. . . . The guarantee of a constitution lies . . . 'in the indwelling spirit and the history of the nation.' . . . To make this indwelling spirit subservient to the will of a political party or of an individual leader was impossible to Hegel."[16] Thus Cassirer is persuaded that Hegel was a humanist whose reverence for the dignity of man would have turned him against twentieth-century totalitarianism. His concern with moral obligations and rights and duties supports this interpretation.

The fact nevertheless remains that Hegel can be read as deifying the state. At a time when the full impact of the emergence of nationalism was being felt, Hegel's glorification of the state strengthened and increased the trend line. It is true that he spoke of intermediate institutions such as corporations and localities performing important functions, and it is also true that he assigned normative values to some of these functions. Yet in the end all aspects of society are subordinate to the state. In the United States the full force of nationalism was limited by a network of overlapping loyalties, which held extreme and crusading loyalties in check. Individuals were members of churches, labor unions, service and fraternal organizations, and other social groups. This dispersion of commitments and the denial of total loyalty to any one group held extremism in check.

Yet it has to be said that nationalism was on the rise, competing and eventually overcoming the principle of legitimacy or maintenance of the status quo in Europe. The first full-scale mobilization of the mass of the people in war occurred with the *leveé en masse* introduced during the French Revolution. In the past, those who fought had been mercenaries and paid volunteers. After the French Revolution the idea of military conscription came to be accepted, and its acceptance was linked to the shift in loyalties from the remote and ambiguous symbol of aristocratic rulers and monarchs to the emotional identification of all the people with the nation-state. The change in focus from rulers and monarchs to all the people within the nation-state had far-ranging effects. In place of the ruler's declaration *l'état c'est moi* (I am the state), the new rallying cry was popular sovereignty and for the French *liberté, égalité, et fraternité* (liberty, equality, and brotherhood). Napoleon helped to plant the seeds of nationalism throughout Europe, and writers

16. Ernst Cassirer, *The Myth of the State* (New Haven, 1946), 273–74, 274 ff.

schooled in the Enlightenment provided some of the intellectual foundations for modern nationalism.

Thus Hegel's idea of the state found a hospitable environment in a Europe that was friendly to its major tenets at least during part of the nineteenth and a fateful segment of the twentieth century. Interpreters have speculated regarding the sources of Hegel's theory of the state. One possible contributing factor may have been his early grounding in Lutheran theology. Although the quiescence of Lutherans in politics can be overstated—for example, Pastor Niemöller was one of the most courageous foes of Hitler—there is some truth in the assertion that the Lutheran faith gave full authority to the state in the realm of politics and limited the role of the Lutheran church to matters of faith and morals. Some critics have tried to argue that Hegel found a substitute for God in the supreme authority and virtue assigned to the state.

Whatever explanatory system we employ to account for Hegel's view of the state, his political theory must be an element in any overall view of nineteenth- and twentieth-century nationalism. Modern man has had difficulty in knowing what to think about nationalism. Sometimes he has claimed too much for nationalism and the nation-state, and sometimes he has been willing to prophesy that nationalism was an archaism or a passing phase in international relations. Even the great historian and scholar Arnold J. Toynbee praised nationalism as the highest expression of civilization in the 1920s but denounced it in the 1940s and 1950s as an obstacle to peace and universalism. For Hegel, the nation-state was in fact universalism as one favored nation-state, Prussia, towered above all others at the pinnacle of the European world only to experience eventually its decline and fall. Eventually some other nation-state, Hegel predicted, would take Prussia's place and become the highest expression of reason and the political and moral order, although no one at the time he wrote could predict which state would rise to such prominence.

In recent years, the brilliant young historian and state department official Francis Fukuyama has analyzed another dimension in Hegel's thinking. He maintains that the German philosopher, in an essay entitled "The End of History," put forward a vision appropriate to the end of the Cold War. For centuries history had followed its tortured course, but in the nineteenth century it reached an end in the emergence of the German state according to

Fukuyama or in the preeminence of Prussia as interpreted by others. History had reached a climax and come to an end with German statehood and culture. All the great tasks of civilization had been accomplished—free enterprise and social security, individual rights and limited social welfare, and the arts and history. Civilization had soared to unprecedented heights. What remained was a small amount of improvement of society, or tidying up at the margins, but the larger ends of mankind had been realized. What matters for this discussion of Hegel is that Fukuyama and others find the basis for their views concerning the end of history in Hegel's writings. Interpreters from this school of thought have less to say about Hegel and totalitarianism. Indeed, some of them deny any connection. They see the German state as the *summum bonum* of civilization, not its corruption. The German state is the forerunner of the West's triumph over communism in the Cold War. Its economic and cultural attainments are proof of the possibility of bringing about the end of history.

The question that remains regarding Hegel's view of the nation-state is whether he assigns it an inordinate measure of virtue, omnipotence, and omniscience. In rescuing the nation-state from Kant's cosmopolitanism, does he claim too much for it at the expense of other counterbalancing forces in society? How well does he demonstrate that reason and the world spirit in history constitute the core of the Prussian state, making it the chosen site for the end of history? And to what extent is this mode of thinking an invitation to Hitler and national socialism in Germany? To level such a charge at a great philosopher such as Hegel or even to pose the question may appear a gross injustice. However, the question does not answer itself. It simply points a direction for future analysis. It is a question every student of political theory and international relations must ask. To those who challenge the inclusion of Hegel in a volume on the fathers of international relations, his views on the nation-state provide the justification. To those who characterize Hegel's writings as abstruse or incomprehensible with little to say of contemporary relevance for international relations, his views on the nation-state constitute an answer. No question is more fundamental than the future of nationalism. Does utopian nationalism by a great power take on the character of a political religion? Can we say that Hegel throws light on the question? The issue of the hegemonic and all-powerful state is still with us. What can we glean from Hegel on this question? Who are the great philosophers of the ages? Some place Hegel alongside Plato, Aristotle, Rousseau, and Marx. In this sense a reading of Hegel, however demanding, may shed light on one of the great unanswered questions of mankind.

Karl Marx (1818–1883)

The twin pillars of Hegel's thought, as we have seen, are, first, idealization of the nation-state and nationalism, which some have said led to fascism and national socialism, and, second, the dialectical method, which as modified by Marx issued in communism. The third connection deserving mention, which proceeds from the first, is the idea of history as following a seemingly inevitable progression from one stage of consciousness to the next, each producing new forms of social and political organization. Each phase of history has a beginning, a middle, and an end. For Hegel the march of reason and the world spirit has carried humanity from slave-owning to theocratic to democratic-egalitarian societies. For Marx the movement is from feudal to industrial to capitalist to socialist economies and is driven by class conflict, not idealism as in the case of Hegel. The vanguard of history preparatory to the final historical stage was Napoleon for Hegel and the proletariat for Marx. Progressive history began with Rousseau, who cried out that man is born free but is everywhere in chains. Only by throwing off the shackles imposed by social institutions will man regain his pristine virtue. It continued with Hegel's vision of the world spirit incarnate in a nation-state. Marx substituted the means of production and the economic system for the idea of the world spirit.

In the long run, the third transformation may have been the most profound. The Greeks saw history as the unfolding of moral principle. History was informed by certain transcendent and objective truths with justice and virtue enshrined in the ideal state outside history. For Christians such as Augustine ultimate truth was reserved for the City of God, which had reality beyond history. Man was redeemed by faith and the grace of God. By contrast, modern progressive history depends not on some transcendent principle of evaluation but on an immanent principle of evaluation located within the bounds of history. For Rousseau the general will is the sole determinant of good and evil. For Hegel, purpose in history finds expression in the idea of the world spirit become incarnate in the German nation-state. For Marx, history is a story of linear moral progress driven by economic and technological change. History in Marxist science moves irresistibly from one stage of development to the next. In the same manner that feudalism had proven superior to primitive societies, capitalism was superior to feudalism. The measure of progress for Marxism was the transformation of material structures and values. Morality is judged not by transcendent principles or the Ten Commandments but by economic standards as defined by Marxist science and existing wholly within history. One stage in history follows inescapably from the preceding one, and each is necessary and inevitable. Whoever is a true believer in the Marxist faith must cooperate with its unfolding historical process, not through supporting premature revolutions or a leader like Mao Tse-tung in a vast and populous country unprepared for revolution, but by assisting the emergence of forces and groups who are in the vanguard of the Marxist-Leninist creed.

Marx began his career as a student of Hegel's writings in Bonn and Berlin. By then Hegelians were divided into two schools of thought: idealism and materialism. Ludwig Feuerbach was the chief protagonist of the latter school, and although as a thinker he was a minor figure compared with Hegel, Marx credits him with freeing Hegelianism from its idealist mystifications. Marx appropriated Feuerbach's views and developed the central thesis that the means of production are the foundation on which the institutional and ideological superstructure of a society are built. However, Marx is too rich and many-sided a thinker to deserve the name of materialistic determinist. He put too much emphasis on the individual's role in shaping change to be called a pure and mechanistic determinist.

Marx's writings are both extensive and varied. His early writings include his *Doctoral Dissertation and Notes* (1839–41), a *Critique of Hegel's "Philosophy of Right"* (1844), *Critique of Hegel's "Philosophy of Law," Theses on Feuerbach, German Ideology,* and the critically important *Economic and Philosophic Manuscripts of 1844,* written when the author was twenty-six but discovered only in

1932.[17] His later writings include *Outline of the Critique of Political Economy* (1859), *The Communist Manifesto* (1848), *The Critique of the Gotha Program* (1875, published in 1891), and *Das Kapital,* or *Capital: A Critique of Political Economy* (Marx was the author of Volume I [1867]; Friedrich Engels wrote Volume II [1885] and Volume III [1894]).

A core idea for Marx was that of the class struggle. Marx discovered the idea in the historical writings of Augustin Thierry on the French Revolution and in David Ricardo on distribution. However, French writers, Marx charged, saw the end of the class struggle in the victory of the bourgeoisie. He argued that the rise of the working class to prominence was far more important historically, heralding as it did the dictatorship of the proletariat and eventually the abolition of all classes in society. By emphasizing the idealistic aspect of conflict, Hegel had stood the dialectic on its head. Marx proposed to turn it right side up.

The debate over the extent to which Marx was a thoroughgoing materialistic determinist is complicated because of his overriding concern with the alienated individual. He maintained that capitalism has alienated and degraded the individual worker, who finds himself enslaved by an alien force that imposes dehumanizing conditions. Labor produces commodities and is itself a commodity. It is divorced from the products of its labor. Because of the accompanying humiliation, man is free only in his animal functions, such as eating, drinking, and procreating. The nonworker, or capitalist, is the main source of the plight of the exploited. The product of a man's labor belongs to persons other than the workers. The worker is alienated not only from his work but from other men as well. The system creates mutual alienation and anxiety, but all of this will be overcome when private property is eliminated.

According to Marx, the capitalist system is dominated by greed and envy as the immediate physical possession of objects becomes the controlling aim in life. Workers are kept at a minimal level of existence and are disposed of as the producer finds he can add to his profits by substituting machinery for workers. The individual

17. One of the most respected editions of these and other early writings is Tom Bottomore, ed., *Karl Marx* (New York, 1964). Another is Loyd D. Easton and Kurt H. Guddat, eds., *Writings of the Young Marx on Philosophy and Society* (Garden City, N.Y., 1967).

will be restored to genuine human existence only when property is done away with and threats to true social participation such as religion, the family, and the state are destroyed. The essence of humanity is existence in society, which is the foundation of human life. The overcoming of the tyranny of private property will lead to a new type of human being, social man, who will cultivate not only the five senses but practical senses such as willing and loving. A truly humanistic society will develop when mankind has moved through various stages of communism, including "raw" or "crude" communism, in which force and coercion are still required. In the various stages of change, some elements of capitalism will persist, including the state. The movement to true communism will be long and tortuous.

In *The Communist Manifesto,* Marx and Engels wrote in some detail about the transition to communism. In the first stage of the transition, the proletariat will become the ruling class and will lead the way to a victory for democracy. Marx's democracy has few if any of the characteristics of liberal democracy. It includes no universal suffrage, direct elections, multiparty campaigning, or parliamentary institutions. Such systems, Marx complained, bring about not freedom but unfreedom. True democracy is neither liberal nor populist. It is, rather, a community in which the free development of each provides the basis for the free development of all. The transition to communism involves gradually taking capital and economic power from the bourgeoisie. It entails centralizing the means of production in the state. Especially in advanced countries, it involves such steps as abolishing private property in ownership of land and using the rent for public purposes; introducing a highly progressive income tax; eliminating the right to inheritance; confiscating property of emigrants; centralizing credit in a national bank; and extending control and ownership of factories and the means of production by the state.

When class distinctions have largely disappeared and all production has been concentrated in the hands of the nation as a whole, public power will no longer have a political dimension. Completion of the process will bring about the end of politics and the state. The state will wither away, and the domination of man by man will be replaced by the administration of things. However, none of these changes will occur overnight. For an indefinite period, the old and the new, remnants of the capitalist system and the first signs of a communist order, will coexist temporarily and uneasily side by side. With the overthrow of the small ruling class of monopoly capitalists and the empowering of the dictatorship of the proletariat, the use of capitalism's immense productive capacity and technology for the benefit and emancipation of men everywhere will be possible. The victory of communism on a worldwide basis will be at hand.

The Marxist prophecy of the global triumph of communism overlooked the power of nationalism. Although Marx had mastered the Hegelian dialectic and turned it to his own ends, he failed to understand the other major Hegelian proposition regarding nationalism and the nation-state. In two world wars, Marxian writers prophesied that war would not occur because "the workers of the world would unite." French workers would refuse to fight German workers, and communists and capitalists would understand that they stood on the threshold of a world revolution. In fact, French workers did fight German workers, and the advanced capitalist states that Marx expected would be the first to embrace revolution turned their backs on the communist utopia. It fell to Lenin to amend the Marxist prophecy when he explained that the road to Paris was through Peking. The harsh injustice and cruel exploitation of the poorer countries of Asia and Africa by colonial regimes would generate revolution in what came to be called the Third World. The rich would become richer and the poor poorer, and wars of national liberation and revolution would begin in the poor countries and spread to the advanced nations.

Marxist science also failed to allow for the accidents and contingencies in history and the near impossibility of predicting the course of events. Speaking in Zurich six weeks before the Bolshevik Revolution, Lenin predicted he would not live to see the communist revolution. Whether prophesying for or against radical change, communist leaders proved no more prescient than capitalist ones. Scientific history of a Marxist character ran aground on the same rocks and shoals that had overturned other versions of scientific history. The pretense of Marxist thought that it had created a true *science humaine* was as misplaced as were the claims of other system builders before and after Marx.

It has been possible to argue that Marx would have made adjustments in his theory if he had lived. He himself questioned whether there could be true "Marxists." He was uncertain about his followers' ability to fully comprehend his theory. By implication, this proposition suggests that not the high priest but the functionaries have erred and been at fault. Critics of Marx, however, point to contradictions, inconsistencies, and omissions in his philosophy. First, if the social consciousness of a society is the result of its mode of economic production, how does Marx explain the emergence in that self-same system of radical reformers dedicated to change? In other words, if the power of the capitalist system is so overwhelming as to produce total alienation of the individual and emasculation of the essence of being human, whence come the nonalienated or the proletariat?

Second, Marx clearly seeks to maintain a place for both individualism and collectivism. It is the degradation and dehumanization of the lives of individuals that justifies revolution. Yet nowhere does Marx make clear the relation between his sympathy for the individual and his readiness to turn to great mass collectivities, employing cruel and barbaric methods to achieve his ends. How does he reconcile his outpouring of sympathy for the individual with more than Machiavellian use of force and violence?

Third, Marx recognizes that outcomes in the political arena are the result of bitter rivalries and conflicts among social classes. In this he goes liberalism one better because liberalism concentrates almost exclusively on the individual, education, and freedom. Yet Marx confines his awareness of the importance of power in the struggle between groups almost exclusively to class struggles. However, power involves contests and rivalries at every level and among almost all groups. In his obsession with class struggles, this fact seemingly escapes Marx.

Finally, the Marxist utopia, including such rough and ready forms as "raw" communism and the dictatorship of the proletariat, claims ultimate and absolute validity for its tenets. Because of the absolute character of its goals, it justifies the most morally questionable and brutal measures as serving its ends. Lady Astor once asked Stalin to explain the slaughter of five million kulaks by the regime. Stalin responded, "What about the carnage brought about by traffic accidents in your country—and all to no purpose?" The communist utopia and its ends are used to justify the violence, brutality, and terror that have characterized most communist regimes wherever they have exercised power. Communism has provided justification for the most heinous crimes, all in the name of the Marxist dream.

None of this is persuasive to the more devoted followers of Marx, who distinguish between the humane concerns of a great philosopher and the abuse of power by those who govern in his name. Moreover, they remind us that we are evaluating thinkers and not political and social movements. To condemn Marx is as wrong as to indict Jefferson for "rotten boroughs," or political corruption. To this argument, critics respond that the real issue is whether certain moral and intellectual anomalies and deficiencies present in Marxism from its inception help us understand the moral deterioration of Marxist regimes. For example, Marx's claim to absolute truth in the march to a new society where the essence of man's humanity will be restored is illusory. So is the promise of a classless society and the substitution of the administration of things for the domination of man by man. Whereas Hitler explained the killing of six million Jews as a necessary hygienic measure on the route to a Germanic superrace, Marxist-Leninist thinkers excused purges of political opponents and the destruction of small farmers as a required stage in the journey toward a classless society. In the absence of any external objective standard comparable to those of classical and Christian thought, the Marxist utopia reigns supreme. Its goal is absolute and unchallenged. As such, it provides a rationale for actions that would otherwise be judged inhumane. The Marxist utopia justifies inhumane acts in the name of creating a fully human new society. It eradicates millions in order to give birth to the new man. If all this were the work of madmen, it would have little to do with political theory. Unfortunately, the seeds for the deed are to be found in Marx's writings. The words and the philosophy lead to tyranny and the destruction of those who resist "absolute truth."

Epilogue

In introducing *Fathers of International Thought,* we referred to three possible views of the interrelationship of the classics in political theory with international political thought. As we come to the end of our inquiry, evidence mounts that the classics are relevant to the understanding of international politics. Despite the absence of a world state, political theory and international theory share a common universe of discourse. If they suffered from mutual neglect in the 1950s, they show signs of reinforcing each other in the 1990s. It seems clear that political philosophy illuminates historic concepts like authority, justice, community, and power. Political theory throws light on recurrent issues such as the relation between peace and order, morality and politics, equality and freedom, and change and continuity. In summing up, we return to lessons that derive from the political philosophers and political theorists surveyed in this study.

Not surprisingly, those most overlooked in the literature of international relations are the classical political philosophers. It has been assumed that because they wrote about ancient city-states or church and emperor, they have nothing to teach us about international relations. In fact, reading Plato helps us comprehend the meaning and characteristics of justice or proportion, the best regime, morality within and between states, war and the causes of war and conditions of peace, the nature of man and political man, political or practical wisdom, and objective truth. From Aristotle we gain a deeper understanding of regimes: the ideal regime and the best under certain conditions; the defining features of monarchy, aristocracy, and polity and their corruptions, tyranny, oligarchy, and democracy; and the distribution of power between those who govern and the governed, and in particular the role of the middle class. He teaches us about equality, virtue, the innate purpose or *telos* of man and the state, the good citizen and the good man, two concepts of justice, and the state as man's highest community. Augustine's legacy is political realism—the idea of society and government as natural for humanity yet necessarily coercive, the duality of church and state, war as inevitable yet tragic, man created good but corrupted by self-pride, love and justice as ultimate norms, proximate justice as the norm in politics, and the ideal interstate order as a system of small states preserved by the balance of power. By contrast, Thomas Aquinas offers the idea of politics as a noble enterprise, the political community as a natural institution based on reason, self-realization in such communities, law, natural law, and community, and prudence as the highest expression of community.

Beginning in the sixteenth and continuing through the nineteenth century, the writings of the fathers of international thought provide direct and explicit relevance for present-day international relations. Machiavelli was a diplomat and a historian. He wrote about the realities of politics and the do's and don'ts for political success. Grotius is called the father of international law, and today's theorists of international politics sometimes are described as Hobbesian or Lockean. Adam Smith wrote about moral sentiments and commutative justice and was the forerunner of today's normative writers. His *The Wealth of Nations* pioneers laissez faire economics, free-trade policies, and theory on the relation of the individual to the economy. Students go back to David Hume for the classic statement of the balance of power and to Jean-Jacques Rousseau for the idea of the general will as the source of a community's law and morality. Those governments whose political systems are based on checks and balances and separation of powers remember Montesquieu. Edmund Burke's conservatism, respect for experience, and historical empiricism constitute inspiration for traditionalists in foreign policy. Three figures in the nineteenth century stand out: Kant, for his views on republicanism and peace; Hegel, for his dialectical method and view of the nation-state and nationalistic universalism; and Marx, whose claim to scientific truth and intention to construct a communist utopia were used as justification for the abuse of power and acts of violence and terror in the Soviet Union and other communist states.

Taken together, the sixteen political theorists denominated fathers of international thought have bequeathed to posterity a rich legacy of thought that continues to shape the ideas and actions, words and deeds of men and nations. It is a legacy on which the masters of international thought have built. Statesmen and diplomats, whether they know it or not, draw on the wisdom of past thinkers. As Sir Maynard Keynes once observed, every policy maker goes back to the thoughts of some "academic scribbler." Those who aspire to become theorists of international relations must stand on the shoulders of those who have gone before them as fathers and masters of international thought.

Bibliography

Aristotle. *Aristotle on His Predecessors.* Translated by A. E. Taylor. Chicago, 1907.

———. *Aristotle's "Ethics" for English Readers.* Translated by Harris Rackham. Oxford, 1943.

———. *Aristotle's "Politics."* Translated by Hippocrates G. Apostle and Lloyd P. Gerson. Grinnell, Iowa, 1986.

———. *Aristotle's Treatise on Rhetoric.* London, 1900.

———. *The Athenian Constitution: The Eudemian Ethics; On Virtues and Vices.* Cambridge, Mass., 1935.

———. *The Complete Works of Aristotle: The Revised Oxford Translation.* Edited by Jonathan Barnes. Princeton, N.J., 1984.

———. *The Ethics of Aristotle: The Nicomachean Ethics.* Translated by J. A. K. Thomson. Harmondsworth, Eng., 1976.

———. *The Politics.* Edited by Stephen Emerson. New York, 1988.

———. *A Treatise on Government.* Translated by William Ellis. London, 1919.

———. *Works.* Edited by W. D. Ross. Chicago, 1955.

Augustine, Saint, bishop of Hippo. *Against the Academics.* New York, 1951.

———. *Augustine of Hippo: Selected Writings.* New York, 1984.

———. *Augustine on "Romans": Propositions from the Epistle to the Romans, Unfinished Commentary on the Epistle to the Romans.* Edited by Paula Fredriksen Landes. Chico, Calif., 1982.

———. *Basic Writings of Saint Augustine.* Edited by Whitney J. Oates. Grand Rapids, Mich., 1980.

———. *The City of God.* Translated by Marcus Dods. New York, 1950.

———. *Earlier Writings*. Translated by John H. S. Burleigh. Philadelphia, 1953.

———. *The Essential Augustine*. Edited by Vernon J. Bourke. New York, 1964.

———. *Letters of Saint Augustine*. Edited by John Leinenweter. Tarrytown, N.Y., 1992.

———. *Saint Augustine Against the Academicians (Contra Academicos)*. Translated by Sister Mary Patricia Garvey. Milwaukee, 1942.

———. *St. Augustine on the Psalms*. Translated by Scholastica Hebgin and Felicitas Corrigan. Westminster, Md., 1960—.

———. *The Trinity*. Translated by Stephen McKenna. Washington, D.C., 1963.

———. *The Works of Saint Augustine: A Translation for the 21st Century*. Translated by Edmund Hill. Edited by John E. Rotelle. Brooklyn, 1990.

Burke, Edmund. *Burke's Speeches: On American Taxation, On Conciliation with America, & Letter to the Sheriffs of Bristol*. Edited by Francis Guy Selby. Westport, Conn., 1974.

———. *The Correspondence of Edmund Burke*. Edited by Thomas W. Copeland *et al.* 10 vols. Cambridge, Eng., 1958–78.

———. *Edmund Burke on Government, Politics, and Society*. Edited by B. W. Hill. New York, 1976.

———. *Letters, Speeches, and Tracts on Irish Affairs*. New York, 1978.

———. *A Letter to a Member of the National Assembly, 1791*. Oxford, 1990.

———. *On the American Revolution: Selected Speeches and Letters*. Edited by Elliott Robert Barkan. New York, 1966.

———. *Pre-Revolutionary Writings*. Cambridge, Eng., 1992.

———. *Reflections on the Revolution in France and on the Proceedings in Certain Societies in London Relative to That Event*. Baltimore, 1976.

———. *Selected Letters of Edmund Burke*. Edited by Harvey C. Mansfield, Jr. Chicago, 1984.

———. *Selected Writings and Speeches*. Edited by Peter J. Stanlis. Gloucester, Mass., 1968.

Fry, Michael, ed. *Adam Smith's Legacy: His Place in the Development of Modern Economics*. London, 1992.

Grotius, Hugo. *The Freedom of the Seas; or, The Right Which Belongs to the Dutch to Take Part in the East Indian Trade*. Translated by Ralph Van Deman Magoffin. Edited by James Brown Scott. New York, 1916.

———. *Hugo Grotius's Defence of Christian Religion, Against Paganism, Judaism, Mahumetism; Together with Some Account of the Three Former Discourses for God, Christ, Scripture*. Collected and translated by Clement Barksdale. London, 1678. Microform.

———. *The Rights of War and Peace, Including the Law of Nature and of*

Nations. Translated by Archibald Colin Campbell. Washington, D.C., 1901.

———. *The Truth of the Christian Religion*. Translated by John Clarke. Oxford, 1818.

———. *The Truth of Christian Religion: In Six Books*. Translated, with the addition of a seventh book, by Symon Patrick. London, 1694. Microform.

———. *The Truth of the Christian Religion: In Six books corrected and illustrated with notes, by Mr. Le Clerc: To which is added a seventh book concerning this question, what Christian church we ought to join ourselves to, by the said Mr. Le Clerc*. Translated by John Clarke. London, 1729.

Hegel, Georg Wilhelm Friedrich. *The Berlin Phenomenology*. Translated and edited by M. J. Petry. Dordrecht, 1981.

———. *The Christian Religion: Lectures on the Philosophy of Religion, Part III, The Revelatory, Consummate, Absolute Religion*. Translated and edited by Peter C. Hodgson. Missoula, Mont., 1979.

———. *The Difference Between Fichte's and Schelling's System of Philosophy. . . .* Translated by Walter Cerf and H. S. Harris. Albany, 1977.

———. *Elements of "The Philosophy of Right."* Translated by H. B. Nisbet. Edited by Allen W. Wood. Cambridge, Eng. 1991.

———. *Encyclopedia of the Philosophical Sciences in Outline, and Other Critical Writings*. Edited by Ernst Behler. New York, 1990.

———. *Encyclopedia of Philosophy*. Translated by Gustav Emil Mueller. New York, 1959.

———. *Faith and Knowledge*. Translated by Walter Cerf and H. S. Harris. Albany, 1977.

———. *Hegel: The Letters*. Translated by Clark Butler and Christine Seiler. Bloomington, Ind., 1984.

———. *Hegel and the Human Spirit: A Translation of the Jena Lectures on the Philosophy of Spirit (1805–6) with Commentary*. Translated by Leo Rauch. Detroit, 1983.

———. *Hegel on Tragedy*. Edited by Anne and Henry Paolucci. Westport, Conn., 1978.

———. *Hegel Selections*. Edited by M. J. Inwood. New York, 1989.

———. *Hegel's Introduction to Aesthetics: Being the Introduction to the Berlin Aesthetics Lectures of the 1820s*. Translated by T. M. Knox. Oxford, 1979.

———. *Hegel's "Logic," Being Part One of the Encyclopedia of the Philosophical Sciences (1830)*. 3d ed., Oxford, 1975.

———. *Hegel's "Philosophy of Mind": Being Part Three of the Encyclopedia of the Philosophical Sciences (1830)*. Oxford, 1971.

———. *Hegel's "Philosophy of Nature."* Translated and edited by M. J. Petry. London, 1970.

———. *Hegel's "Philosophy of Right."* Translated by T. M. Knox. London, 1967.

———. *Hegel's "Science of Logic."* Translated by A. V. Miller. London, 1969.

———. *Introduction to "The Lectures on the History of Philosophy."* Translated by T. M. Knox and A. V. Miller. Oxford, 1985.

———. *Introduction to "The Philosophy of History" with Selections from "The Philosophy of Right."* Translated by Leo Rauch. Indianapolis, 1988.

———. *The Jena System, 1804–5: Logic and Metaphysics.* Translation edited by John W. Burbidge and George di Giovanni. Kingston, 1986.

———. *The Phenomenology of Mind.* Translated by J. B. Baillie. London, 1977.

———. *Phenomenology of Spirit.* Translated by A. V. Miller. Oxford, 1977.

———. *The Philosophy of History.* Translated by J. Sibree. New York, 1944.

Hobbes, Thomas. *Aristotle's Treatises on Rhetoric, Literally Translated.* London, 1900.

———. *Clarendon Edition of the Philosophical Works of Thomas Hobbes.* Oxford, 1983—.

———. *A Dialogue Between a Philosopher and a Student of the Common Laws of England.* Edited by Joseph Cropsey. Chicago, 1971.

———. *The Elements of Law, Natural & Politic.* Edited by Ferdinand Tonnies. Cambridge, Eng., 1928.

———. *The English Works of Thomas Hobbes of Malmesbury.* 11 vols. Edited by Sir William Molesworth. London, 1839–45.

———. *The History of the Civil Wars of England from the Year 1640 to 1660.* London, 1679.

———. *Hobbes's "Leviathan."* Oxford, 1952.

———. *Leviathan.* Edited by Richard Tuck. Cambridge, Eng., 1991.

———. *The Life of Mr. Thomas Hobbes of Malmesbury, and Thomae Hobbesii Malmesburiensis Vita.* Exeter, Eng., 1979.

Hume, David. *Dialogues Concerning Natural Religion: In Focus.* London, 1991.

———. *An Enquiry Concerning Human Understanding, and Other Essays.* New York, 1963.

———. *An Enquiry Concerning the Principles of Morals.* Indianapolis, 1983.

———. *Essays Moral, Political, and Literary.* Edited by T. H. Green and T. H. Grose. London, 1899.

———. *Essays Moral, Political, and Literary.* Indianapolis, 1987.

———. *The History of England: From the Invasion of Julius Caesar to the Revolution in 1688.* Chicago, 1975.

———. *Hume on Religion.* Edited by Richard Wollheim. Cleveland, 1964.

———. *The Letters of David Hume*. Edited by J. Y. T. Greig. Oxford, 1969.

———. *A Treatise of Human Nature*. 2nd ed. Oxford, 1978.

Kant, Immanuel. *Anthropology from a Pragmatic Point of View*. Translated by Victor Lyle Dowdell. Edited by Hans H. Rudnick. Carbondale, Ill., 1978.

———. *Cambridge Edition of the Works of Immanuel Kant*. Cambridge, Eng., 1992—.

———. *The Critique of Judgement*. Translated by J. H. Bernard. New York, 1966.

———. *The Critique of Practical Reason, and Other Writings in Moral Philosophy*. Translated and edited by Lewis White Beck. New York, 1976.

———. *Critique of Pure Reason*. Translated by Wolfgang Schwarz. Aelen, 1982.

———. *"Eternal Peace": and Other International Essays*. Translated by W. Hastic. Ann Arbor, Mich., 1981.

———. *Ethical Philosophy: The Complete Texts of "Grounding for the Metaphysics of Morals" and "Metaphysical Principles of Virtue," Part II of "The Metaphysics of Morals."* Translated by James W. Ellington. Indianapolis, 1983.

———. *Foundations of the Metaphysics of Morals*. Translated by Lewis White Beck. Indianapolis, 1969.

———. *Kant: Political Writings*. Translated by H. B. Nisbet. Edited by Hans Reiss. Cambridge, Eng., 1991.

———. *Kant's Critical Philosophy for English Readers*. 2 vols. London, 1888–1915.

———. *Lectures on Logic*. Translated and edited by J. Michael Young. Cambridge, Eng., 1992.

———. *Logic*. Translated by Robert S. Hartman and Wolfgang Schwarz. Indianapolis, 1974.

———. *The Metaphysical Elements of Justice: Part I of "The Metaphysics of Morals."* Translated by John Ladd. Indianapolis, 1965.

———. *Metaphysical Foundations of Natural Science*. Translated by James Ellington. Indianapolis, 1970.

———. *The Metaphysics of Morals*. Translated by Mary Gregor. Cambridge, Eng. 1991.

———. *The Moral Law: Kant's Groundwork of "The Metaphysic of Morals."* Translated by H. J. Paton. 1976; rpr. London, 1991.

———. *On History*. Translated by Lewis White Beck *et al.* Edited by Lewis White Beck. Indianapolis, 1963.

———. *Perpetual Peace*. Translated by M. Campbell Smith. London, 1903.

———. *"Perpetual Peace" and Other Essays on Politics, History, and Morals*. Translated by Ted Humphrey. Indianapolis, 1983.

———. *Principles of Lawful Politics: Immanuel Kant's Philosophic Draft Toward "Eternal Peace."* Translated by Wolfgang Schwarz. Aalen, 1988.

———. *Theoretical Philosophy, 1755–1770.* Translated and edited by David Walford. Cambridge, Eng., 1992.

———. *What Real Progress Has Metaphysics Made in Germany Since the Time of Leibniz and Wolff?* Translated by Ted Humphrey. New York, 1983.

Locke, John. *An Essay Concerning Human Understanding.* Oxford, 1979.

———. *Essays on the Law of Nature.* Oxford, 1954.

———. *A Letter Concerning Toleration: In Focus.* London, 1991.

———. *Locke on Politics, Religion, and Education.* Edited by Maurice Cranston. New York, 1965.

———. *A Paraphrase and Notes on the Epistles of St. Paul to the Galatians, 1 and 2 Corinthians, Romans, Ephesians.* Edited by Arthur W. Wainwright. 2 vols. Oxford, 1987.

———. *Questions Concerning the Law of Nature.* Ithaca, 1990.

———. *The Reasonableness of Christianity, with a Discourse of Miracles, and Part of a Third Letter Concerning Toleration.* Edited by I. T. Ramsey. Stanford, 1958.

———. *The Second Treatise of Government.* New York, 1986.

———. *Some Thoughts Concerning Education.* Edited by John W. and Jean S. Yolton. Oxford, 1989.

———. *Two Treatises of Government.* Edited by Peter Laslett. Cambridge, Eng., 1988.

———. *Two Treatises of Government: A Critical Edition with an Introduction and Apparatus Criticus by Peter Laslett.* 2nd ed. Cambridge, Eng., 1970.

Machiavelli, Niccolò. *The Art of War.* Edited by Neal Wood. Indianapolis, 1965.

———. *The Art of War. In Seven Books.* Albany, 1815.

———. *The Letters of Machiavelli: A Selection.* Translated and edited by Allan Gilbert. New York, 1961.

———. *The Living Thoughts of Machiavelli.* Translated by Doris E. Troutman and Arthur Livingston. Edited by Carlo Sforza. New York, 1940.

———. *Mandragola.* Translated by Mera J. Flaumenhaft. Prospect Heights, Ill., 1981.

———. *The Portable Machiavelli.* New York, 1979.

———. *The Prince.* Translated by Harvey C. Mansfield, Jr. Chicago, 1985.

———. *"The Prince" and "The Discourses."* New York, 1940.

———. *The Works of Nicholas Machiavel, Secretary of State to the Republic of Florence.* London, 1762.

Marx, Karl. *Capital: A Critique of Political Economy.* Translated by Ben Fowkes. New York, 1977.

———. *The Class Struggles in France, 1848–1850.* Translated by Henry Kuhn. New York, 1924.

———. *The Communist Manifesto.* Mattituck, N.Y., 1977.

———. *Early Writings.* Translated and edited by T. B. Bottomore. New York, 1964.

———. *Economic and Philosophic Manuscripts of 1844.* London, 1975. Vol. III of Karl Marx and Frederick Engels, *Collected Works.*

———. *The Essential Marx: The Non-economic Writings, a Selection.* Edited by Saul K. Padover. New York, 1979.

———. *Essential Writings of Karl Marx.* Edited by David Cante. New York, 1967.

———. *Karl Marx.* Edited by Tom Bottomore. New York, 1964.

———. *Karl Marx: Essential Writings.* Edited by Frederic L. Bender. New York, 1972.

———. *Karl Marx and Frederick Engels: Selected Correspondence (1843–1895).* Moscow, 1956.

———. *Karl Marx, Frederick Engels: Collected Works.* 30 vols. projected. London 1975—.

———. *Writings of the Young Marx on Philosophy and Society.* Edited by Loyd D. Easton and Kurt H. Guddat. Garden City, N.Y., 1967.

Montesquieu, Charles de Secondat, baron de. *Considerations on the Causes of the Greatness of the Romans and Their Decline.* Translated by David Lowenthal. New York, 1965.

———. *The Persian Letters.* Translated by C. J. Betts. Harmondsworth, Eng., 1973.

———. *The Political Theory of Montesquieu.* Translated by Melvin Richter. Cambridge, Eng., 1977.

———. *The Spirit of the Laws.* Translated and edited by Anne M. Cohler. Cambridge, Eng., 1989.

———. *The Spirit of the Laws: A Compendium of the First English Edition.* Edited by David Wallace Carrithers. Berkeley, 1977.

Plato. *Apology, Crito, Phaedo, Symposium, Republic.* Translated by B. Jowett, edited by Louise Ropes Loomis. New York, 1942.

———. *The Apology of Plato, with a Revised Text and English Notes, and a Digest of Platonic Idioms.* Edited by James Riddell. New York, 1973.

———. *The Collected Dialogues of Plato, Including the Letters.* Edited by Edith Hamilton and Huntington Cairns. Princeton, N.J., 1961.

———. *The Dialogues of Plato.* Edited by William Chase Greene. New York, 1932.

———. *The Dialogues of Plato.* Translated by R. E. Allen. New Haven, 1984—.

———. *The Laws of Plato.* Translated by Thomas L. Panafe. New York, 1980.

———. *The Laws of Plato.* Translated by A. E. Taylor. London, 1934.
———. *The Republic.* Edited by Charles M. Bakewell. New York, 1928.
———. *The Republic.* Edited by Raymond Larson. Arlington Heights, Ill., 1979.
———. *The Republic.* Translated by Richard W. Sterling and William C. Scott. New York, 1985.
Rousseau, Jean-Jacques. *The Confessions of Jean-Jacques Rousseau.* Translated by J. M. Cohen. Baltimore, 1953.
———. *Discourse on the Origins of Inequality (Second Discourse); Polemics; and Political Economy.* Translated by Judith R. Bush *et al.* Edited by Roger Masters and Christopher Kelly. Hanover, N.H., 1992.
———. *Discourse on the Sciences and Arts (First Discourse); and Polemics.* Translated by Judith R. Bush *et al.* Edited by Roger Masters and Christopher Kelly. Hanover, 1992.
———. *Emile; or, On Education.* Translated by Allan Bloom. New York, 1979.
———. *The First and Second Discourses Together with the Replies to Critics and Essay on the Origin of Languages.* Translated and edited by Victor Gourevitch. New York, 1986.
———. *Julie. . . .* Paris, n.d.
———. *La nouvelle Heloise. Julie; or, The New Eloise: Letters of Two Lovers, Inhabitants of a Small Town at the Foot of the Alps.* Translated by Judith H. McDowell. University Park, Pa., 1968.
———. *On the Origin of Inequality; A Discourse on Political Economy.* Chicago, 1949.
———. *Political Writings.* Edited by C. E. Vaughn. New York, 1962.
———. *The Reveries of the Solitary Walker.* Translated by Charles E. Butterworth. New York, 1979.
———. *Rousseau on International Relations.* Edited by Stanley Hoffmann and David P. Fidler. Oxford, 1991.
———. *The Social Contract.* Translated by G. D. H. Cole. Buffalo, 1988.
———. *"The Social Contract," and "Discourses."* Translated by G. D. H. Cole. London, 1973.
Smith, Adam. *Adam Smith Today: An Inquiry into the Nature and Causes of the Wealth of Nations.* Edited by Arthur Hugh Jenkins. Port Washington, N.Y., 1969.
———. *The Correspondence of Adam Smith.* Edited by Ernest Campbell Mossner and Ian Simpson Ross. 2nd ed. Oxford, 1987.
———. *Essays on Philosophical Subjects.* Edited by W. P. D. Wightman and J. C. Bryce. Oxford, 1980.
———. *The Essential Adam Smith.* Edited by Robert L. Heilbroner. New York, 1986.
———. *An Inquiry into the Nature and Causes of the Wealth of Nations.* Edited by Edwin Cannan. Chicago, 1976.

———. *An Inquiry into the Nature and Causes of the Wealth of Nations.* Edited by R. H. Campbell and A. S. Skinner. 2 vols. Oxford, 1976.
———. *Lectures on Jurisprudence.* Edited by R. L. Meck *et al.* Oxford, 1978.
———. *Lectures on Rhetoric and Belles Lettres.* Edited by J. C. Bryce. Oxford, 1983.
———. *The Theory of Moral Sentiments.* Edited by D. D. Raphael and A. L. Macfie. Oxford, 1976.
Thomas Aquinas, Saint. *An Aquinas Reader.* Edited by Mary T. Clark. Garden City, N.Y., 1972.
———. *Aristotle: On Interpretation.* Translated by Jean T. Oesterle. Milwaukee, 1962.
———. *The Political Ideas of St. Thomas Aquinas: Representative Selections.* Edited by Dino Bigongiari. New York, 1966.
———. *The Summa Contra Gentiles of Saint Thomas Aquinas.* London, 1923—.
———. *Summa Theologica.* Westminster, Md., 1981.
———. *Treatise on the Virtues.* Notre Dame, Ind., 1984.
———. *War and Peace.* Washington, D.C., 1982.
Thucydides. *History of the Peloponnesian War.* Translated by Rex Warner. Harmondsworth, Eng., 1954.
———. *"The Peloponnesian War": The Thomas Hobbes Translation.* 2 vols. Edited by David Grene. Ann Arbor, 1959.
Wilbur, James B., and Harold J. Allen, eds. *The Worlds of Hume and Kant.* Buffalo, N.Y., 1982.

Index

Alexander the Great, 36, 37, 43
Althusius, Johannes, 73, 74
Aquinas, Thomas, 3, 17, 44, 54–61, 73, 81, 95, 105
Arendt, Hannah, 4
Aristotle, 3, 16, 36–43, 44, 45, 47, 49, 52–55, 57–62, 64, 66, 73, 76, 96, 120
Aron, Raymond, 95
Augustine, 3, 17, 32, 44–53, 55, 58, 59, 60, 61, 64, 120, 122

Bacon, Francis, 64, 77
Balance of power, 5, 8, 13, 15, 18, 21, 51, 53, 57, 88, 90, 91, 93, 94
Beck, Lewis White, 107, 108
Bentham, Jeremy, 14, 20
Bickel, Alexander M., 101, 102
Bismarck, Otto von, 13
Bolingbroke, 18, 22, 95
Borgia, Cesare, 64
Brecht, Arnold, 4
Bruning, Chancellor Heinrich, 4
Bull, Hedley, 70
Burckhardt, Jakob, 23
Burke, Edmund, 13, 67, 84, 94, 98–103
Butterfield, Herbert, 6, 7, 62

Calvin, John, 60
Canning, George, 13
Carr, E. H., 13
Cassirer, Ernst, 116, 117
Cato, 85, 86
Chicago, University of, 2, 4
Churchill, Winston, 100
Cicero, 50
City of God, 44–49, 52, 53, 55, 60, 61, 120
City of Man, 46, 53
Clausewitz, Karl von, 67
Clement VII, 63
Constitution, U.S., 32, 39
Cromwell, Oliver, 80
Crucé, Emeric, 12

d'Alembert, Jean Le Rond, 94
Dante, 17, 60
Deane, Herbert, 51
Declaration of Independence, 42, 82

Democracy, 8, 20, 27, 29, 33–35, 38, 39, 41–43, 74, 98, 109, 123
Descartes, René, 76, 94, 105
Dewey, John, 28
Dialectical method, 113, 120
Diderot, Denis, 94, 96
Dionysius II of Syracuse, 27
Douglas, Stephen, 42

Engels, Friedrich, 122
Enlightenment, 21, 79, 84, 94, 96, 105, 106, 118
Emerson, Ralph Waldo, 23
Erasmus, 12

Federalist 51, 42
Feuerbach, Ludwig, 121
Fichte, Johann, 12, 113
Fordism, 87
Franklin, Benjamin, 94
Frederick the Great, 12
Frederick II (Holy Roman emperor), 63, 109
French Revolution, 33, 95, 96, 99, 101, 105, 109, 117, 122
Friedrich, Carl J., 4, 30, 97
Fukuyama, Francis, 118, 119

Gibbon, Edward, 94
Glorious Revolution, 20, 80
Gross, Leo, 4
Grotius, 3, 11, 69–76, 110
Guicciardini, Francesco, 93
Gulf War, 2, 21, 93
Gurian, Waldemar, 4

Halifax, Lord, 80, 81
Halle, Louis J., Jr., 3
Hamilton, Alexander, 15, 18, 22, 39, 43, 91, 109
Harrington, James, 67, 95
Hayek, Friedrich von, 4
Hegel, G. W. F., 12, 97, 99, 103, 105, 113–20, 121, 122, 124
Hitler, Adolf, 4, 6, 8, 22, 39, 79, 80, 101, 118, 119, 126
Hobbes, Thomas, 3, 11, 15, 18, 22, 45, 67, 69, 70, 73, 75–85, 95, 97, 108
Holmes, Oliver Wendell, 6, 101
Homer, 30, 77
Hooker, Thomas, 81, 95
Hula, Erich, 4
Hume, David, 13, 15, 18, 84, 87, 89–94, 99, 105
Hussein, Saddam, 2, 22, 94

International law, 3–6, 12, 13, 57, 69–76, 82, 110

James II, 80
Jefferson, Thomas, 18, 27, 39, 91, 94, 126
Jonas, Hans, 4
Jus ad bellum, 71
Jus in bello, 71

Kant, Immanuel, 14, 70, 75, 97, 99, 103–12, 119
Kelsen, Hans, 4
Kirchheimer, Otto, 4

Lasswell, Harold, 34
Lauterpacht, Hersh, 4, 71
League of Nations, 6, 12, 14, 71
Lincoln, Abraham, 39, 42
Lippmann, Walter, 3, 112
Livy, 63
Locke, John, 11, 18, 20, 69, 80–83, 92, 94, 95, 97, 101, 105
Luther, Martin, 60

Machiavelli, Niccolò, 3, 12, 13, 15, 17, 32, 45, 62–68, 70, 75, 91, 93, 125
Mahan, Alfred, 18
Maistre, Joseph de, 11
Mannheim, Karl, 4

Mansfield, Harvey, Jr., 62
Mao Tse-tung, 121
Marx, Karl, 103, 120–26
Masters of International Thought (Thompson), 3, 100
Mattingly, Garrett, 13
Maurice of Nassau, 67
Medici, 63, 64
Meinecke, Friedrich, 12
Melian dialogue, 13, 38
Mersenne, Marin, 77
Mill, John Stuart, 13
Mirabeau, Comte de, 109
Montaigne, Michel de, 94
Montesquieu, 67, 84, 94–96
More, Thomas, 13, 18
Morgenthau, Hans J., 2, 3, 6
Murray, John Courtney, 3, 61

Napoleon, 36, 39, 101, 117, 120
Napoleon III, 39
Napoleonic Wars, 21
Natural law, 48, 52, 56, 58–60, 72–75, 81, 99
Neumann, Franz, 4
Neumann, Sigmund, 4
Niebuhr, Reinhold, 3, 5, 6, 29, 32, 46, 52, 59, 60, 61, 100, 101, 109, 111, 114

Oldenbarnevele, John van, 70
Oppenheim, Lassa, 71, 72, 76

Pact of Paris (1928), 71, 111
Penn, William, 12, 14
Pericles, 26, 34
Philip of Macedon, 27
Philip IV of France, 63
Plato, 3, 19, 26–35, 36, 37, 40, 45, 47, 49, 53, 64, 73, 79, 95, 98, 106, 120
Platonism, 29
Plutarch, 63
Polybius, 63, 66, 91
Popper, Karl, 29
Pufendorf, Samuel, 12, 75, 110

Raison d'état, 66
Ranke, Leopold, 12, 13
Reformation, 81
Republicanism, 62, 68, 80, 109, 112
Riessler, Kurt, 4
Roman Empire, 16, 47, 50, 55, 94
Rousseau, Jean-Jacques, 13, 45, 84, 92, 94–99, 101, 120, 121
Rusk, Dean, 36

Sabine, George H., 24
St. Pierre, Abbé de, 12
Salisbury, Lord, 13
Schiffer, Walter, 56
Schumpeter, Joseph A., 4
Schwarzenberger, George, 4
Seeley, Sir John, 13
Socrates, 27, 28, 32, 33, 34, 37, 113
Sophists, 28, 37
Spier, Hans, 4
Spinoza, Benedict de, 46, 67, 75
Stalin, Joseph, 39, 79, 80, 125
Strauss, Leo, 4, 23, 24, 30, 31, 62
Suárez, Francisco, 73
Sully, Duc de, 14

Tacitus, 63
Telos, 40, 41, 55, 65
Thierry, Augustin, 122
Thucydides, 13, 27, 37, 77, 91
Tocqueville, Alexis de, 2, 67
Townshend, Charles, 84
Toynbee, Arnold, 2, 57, 118
Treitschke, Heinrich von, 12
Turgot, Anne-Robert-Jacques, 87, 94

Vattel, Emmerich von, 12, 110
Viner, Jacob, 4, 86

Visscher, Charles de, 76
Voegelin, Eric, 4
Voltaire, 85, 94

Wight, Martin, 10, 11, 12, 18, 20, 32, 70
William of Occam, 77
Wilson, Woodrow, 5, 16, 28, 112
Wilsonianism, 21
Wolfers, Arnold, 5, 6, 14–19, 21
Wriston, Henry, 8

Xenophon, 63